T0342460

# Mediated Narration in the Digital Age

**Frontiers of Narrative**   SERIES EDITOR

*Jesse E. Matz*, Kenyon College

# Mediated Narration in the Digital Age

*Storying the Media World*

PETER JOSEPH GLOVICZKI

University of Nebraska Press | Lincoln

Library of Congress Cataloging-in-Publication Data
Names: Gloviczki, Peter Joseph, author.
Title: Mediated narration in the digital age: storying
the media world / Peter Joseph Gloviczki.
Description: Lincoln: University of Nebraska Press,
[2021]
Series: Frontiers of narrative | Includes
bibliographical references and index.
Identifiers: LCCN 2020057440
ISBN 9781496217639 (hardback)
ISBN 9781496228369 (epub)
ISBN 9781496228376 (pdf)
Subjects: LCSH: Storytelling in mass media—Case
studies. | Digital storytelling—United States—Case
studies. | Online journalism—United States—Case
studies. | Narration (Rhetoric)—Case studies. |
BISAC: SOCIAL SCIENCE / Media Studies |
LANGUAGE ARTS & DISCIPLINES / Journalism
Classification: LCC P96.S78 G568 2021 |
DDC 302.23—dc23
LC record available at
https://lccn.loc.gov/2020057440

Set in Minion Pro by Mikala R. Kolander.

*Dedicated to the memory of Dr. Hazel F. Dicken-Garcia, my first teacher of mass media history*

*A more sophisticated concept of news, consistent with dialogical ethics, is authentic disclosure. In this perspective, reporting must be grounded historically and biographically, so that complex cultures are represented adequately.*

CLIFFORD CHRISTIANS


*We don't have a right to ask whether we're going to succeed or not. The only question we have a right to ask is: What's the right thing to do? What does this earth require of us, if we want to continue to live on it?*

WENDELL BERRY

# Contents

# Tables

# Acknowledgments

Thank you to the lovely Jenny, for the time, space, and understanding to write as I completed this manuscript. To my parents: Thank you for always being there for me. To Dr. Ryan, Chris, Paige, and Paiton Higgins: Thank you beyond measure, always for everything. To Nicholas Gabrielson: Thank you for always reminding me what I can do. Thank you to Dr. Lana Rakow, for recommending reading material early on in my writing process. Thank you to Elise McHugh, for reading over the proposal for this book and helping me format it correctly.

Thanks to the University of Iowa's Obermann Center for Advanced Studies, for a lovely week in March 2018 as a visiting fellow, which allowed me time to work on the proposal that became this book.

Thank you to Dr. Shayla Thiel-Stern, for comments on an earlier version of this book; to Dr. Kasi Williamson, for reading an early draft of this book; and to Elizabeth Turner, for magical skills in document conversion.

I wish to gratefully acknowledge the support of the South Carolina Independent Colleges and Universities (SCICU), which graciously provided financial support for my travel to the University of Iowa, where I spent a week at the Obermann Center for Advanced Studies.

I hope this book reaches students and scholars everywhere. Particular acknowledgment is due to the Minnesota Hungarians around me, whose positivity and good cheer have reminded me, time and again, of the pleasures of intercultural identities and experiences.

Mediated Narration in the Digital Age

# Storying as an Active Process

The foundations of this inquiry lie in Norman K. Denzin's admonition to "always write out of those spaces and experiences that carry the sting of memory, those epiphanies, and turning point moments that leave a mark on you" (2011, par. 2). Denzin's words guide what follows. The theories presented, methods employed, cases chosen, analysis provided, and conclusions reached are each influenced by a critical, poststructuralist position I have found in Denzin's formulation.

The title of this book, *Mediated Narration in the Digital Age*, was chosen for three reasons:

(1) I position storying as an active process: it is dynamic and in a state of becoming. Storying is a deeply human and humane process that existed before me and will progress after me. I consider it a privilege, as a scholar-teacher, to write about it. In writing about it, I am also inevitably placing myself within it and forcing myself to be influenced by it. I have attempted throughout to be as transparent, open, and detailed as possible about how the research process has influenced me. I include the autoethnographic vignettes at the beginning of each chapter in an attempt to admit and recognize my position within the work. Even though my position within the text is inevitable—every author is always in their own text—I assert that the author's position in any story—indeed, my position in this story—represents an asset to and for the work. Storying self into other strengthens the resulting dialogue. To be able to write about any dynamic process of becoming, one needs to enforce some boundaries. I have chosen the time period studied in this text (1991–2018) because it is an accessible way to story self into other and memory into media.

(2) The chosen time period also straddles a massive technological change, the rise and development of the internet, that continues to reorganize journalism and mass communication. Just as storying is an active process that is dynamic and in a state of becoming, so too are journalism and mass communication. The seven cases studied herein, individually and taken together, work to make sense of and bring meaning to that change. I employ the case study research strategy to point to the identifiable core of that change. Accordingly, to be storying the media world at this moment is an apt way of understanding our present-day sociocultural transition of human into machine and machine back into/onto human. It is worth noting that, even within these spatial and temporal boundaries, there is nothing decisive about either 1991 or 2018. On the front end, the internet has much deeper roots than that (see, for example, Licklider and Taylor [1968]). And on the back end, the ongoing changes not only reflect today: technological change will likely continue into the foreseeable future, for years and even decades to come.

(3) Mediated narration concerns how the story is told. To mediate a story is to make it available through print, broadcast, and/or digital channels, and to narrate a story is to tell it. Mediated narration is the practice of doing both of those things at the same time, with the intended purpose of both transmitting that story/ies but also, and even more importantly, of influencing the cultures that are audiences for the story. The audience is an active one that will *and must* reposition and influence the story back to its producers as well. Textual analysis is thus certainly a blend of researcher and researched in an ongoing, never-ending dialogue. Therefore mediated narration, like storying and the media world, respectively, is also always active, dynamic, and in a state of becoming. Finally, the digital age is both an affordance and a constraint. As I take care to make clear throughout the text, digital platforms and practices bring new opportunities and new responsibilities to and for mediated narration. To study mediated narration in the time period considered in this book is necessarily to study and be immersed within the digital age.

The purpose of this book is to use autoethnography, the case study research strategy, and textual analysis in order to better understand the implications of mediated narration on the process of storying the media world.

## Representation and the Public

This book examines representation and the public. I am interested in the way ethics emphasize certain representations. I am interested in how case studies reveal, often unexpectedly, who or what is represented. I am interested in how autoethnography stories the self into social representation. I am interested in the ways textual analysis of various media explores what is represented and how it is represented. This inquiry marks the coming together of each of those elements. I hold representation as important because it makes public what should be valued in social, cultural, political, and economic terms. The process of making representation public—of sharing representation with a public audience—builds, sustains, reinforces, and legitimizes the representation until such time that the representation is considered common sense, effectively solidifying the representation as what is normal in and for the human experience. Once a representation is broadly considered normal in the everyday imagination, it becomes difficult to delegitimize or even question it, because institutional or individual forces usually do not wish to upset the established order, especially if and when that established order serves to bolster or protect their material and practical interests.

I take the position that humans are necessarily relational beings. As Ellis, Adams, and Bochner articulate, "We live connected to social networks that include friends and relatives, partners and children, co-workers and students, and we work in universities and research facilities" (2011, par. 28). Importantly, the social networks that these authors are referring to are social networks in the broadest sense, which is to say those that encompass both online and offline interactions. The work of living is also the work of socialization. To live is to be socialized in a specific way, depending on the conditions we find ourselves in, or place ourselves into, in the world. Where, how, with whom, and when we live each carries social consequences. Each of these variables represents the social context of and for our lives. These social-context variables matter because we choose to engage them through the work of our living. We *use* our online and offline social networks to afford ourselves opportunities to get along, and get ahead, in everyday life. It is worth noting that I do not consider use in a negative sense; I am stating that use is a necessity of living. Our attitudes, behaviors, and practices—in sum, how we use our context—has consequences. To understand anything about the consequences, one must delve into the realities of the human experience. In this inquiry I aim to undertake some of that work.

One of the social tools we relate through are the various media that we consume across our everyday lives. In the early 1970s Katz, Blumler, and Gurevitch stated, "Media researchers ought to be studying human needs to discover how much the media do or do not contribute to their creation and satisfaction" (1973, 521). Inspired by Katz, Blumler, and Gurevitch, I begin from the premise that media consumption can influence the ways we conceptualize the world around us, especially when we lack first-hand experience with what is being mediated. Humans learn to relate to the unknown, at least in part, through their limited knowledge of it. Accordingly, what is mediated, and how and why it is mediated, may influence individuals' attitudes about the topics being consumed.

As Gerbner and Gross noted: "The environment that sustains the most distinctive aspects of human existence is the environment of symbols. We learn, share, and act upon meanings derived from that environment" (1976, 173). We are, and have long been, influenced by our media consumption. It has, in fact, been an integral part of our everyday lived "environments" for some time. Like Gerbner and Gross, I recognize any environment as extraordinarily broad and expansive, too numerous to capture in its entirety. Environments can be difficult to study precisely because we are immersed within them. It is the sense of immersion, in fact, that makes them so important to study.

I have recognized this phenomenon in the classroom as well. I ask my students, often at the beginning of a new term, to relay their earliest memories associated with the media. Inevitably, they will share about a certain show or a certain song or a certain crisis moment, and then I will do the same. Though the particulars of our sharing may be different, the symbolic power of what is shared tends to be fairly constant. As many symbolic interactionists have noted much more eloquently than I, the symbols that populate our worlds also help construct our worlds. My anecdotal experiences, and those of my students, lend support to Gerbner and Gross's overarching conception of the significance of our environment. We often carry the symbolic power of our lived experiences with us, without necessarily realizing the extent to which we might be being shaped by them.

Gerbner and Gross recognized that medium change was likely over time. Their focus was on television, but they were aware of the potential for novel media to emerge, as occurred with the rise and development of social media platforms. They note, "New technologies on the horizon may enrich the choices of the choosy but cannot replace the simultaneous public experience of a common symbolic environment that now binds diverse communities" (1976, 173). Following Gerbner and Gross, I am interested in where the "simultaneous public experience" has traveled from 1991 through 2018 and what it has meant to engage in that experience, with particular attention to mediated narration.

Two conceptual questions drive my work:

1) How are stories being narrated? I use the tools of qualitative research, especially the case study research strategy, autoethnography, and textual analysis to investigate that question.
2) What might be the impact on the audience of narrating stories in that way? I am employing a critical, poststructuralist theoretical lens to investigate that question.

I ask these conceptual questions with a sense of gratitude toward Gerbner and Gross, especially to Gerbner, whose work on cultivation theory has stimulated my thinking about communication and media studies. His ideas have helped me recognize and begin to grapple with media as lived experience. Following Gerbner, with considerable dialogic influence from Ellis, Adams, and Bochner (2011), I take the position that media influence audiences (and audiences also influence media). I set out to better discern the particulars of that influence. Even though this book does not employ cultivation theory directly, that theory is certainly in the background of all of my critical inquiry. The theory I utilize in this book is best termed critical theory.

Critical theory broadly attempts to point to existing power structures, both hidden and visible, to make plain how they function and, to the extent that it can be discerned, why they function in the ways they do. Critical theory is critical because it works to unearth what some may prefer, as an exercise in power, to keep shrouded. Power is always on the market, which is to say it is being traded between buyers (those who want it) and sellers (those who have it). The more complicated the terms of the market are—in other words, the harder it is to understand, access, and participate in the market—the more likely the market is to progress undisturbed and, in doing so, to consolidate its influence. One example of upending the established order would be the way that John Bogle popularized broad market index funds for individual investors on the U.S. stock market, especially through the Vanguard 500 Stock Market Index Fund and, later, the Vanguard Total Stock Market Index Fund (see, for example, Bogle). The somewhat closed community of stock market investing became somewhat more open. Critical theory often works toward and hopes for similarly incremental change. Through our participation in the human experience we are regularly, if not always, engaging in power relations. As an example: if we are an employee, we must sleep at night in order to be able to go to work the next morning, so that we can receive money to pay for our lives. In this way, we trade time for money. We sleep in preparation for our work and we work in order to be able to earn. There is nothing inherently wrong with doing so: we may enjoy our work and we may enjoy the money that our time has earned us, but the power dynamic is what ultimately governs how we spend our time.

In this inquiry I study mediated narration. As noted earlier, mediated narration is how stories are told through media outlets. Narration in this context might refer to various aspects of storytelling, but I am most interested in what is spoken on television, what is written in newspapers, and what is visualized on film in mediated narration. I hope to help journalists recognize and interrogate the patterns and formulae that, rightly or wrongly, tend to undergird their media work. I hope also to help students and scholars make sense of the affordances and constraints embedded in those practices. I call for more communitarian storytelling practices in mediated narration because the cases examined here strongly suggest that there has become an established, normalized, reductive strategy of mediated narration by media authors. At the same time, there has become an acceptance of, or compliance with, this strategy by audiences. In our digital age we not only can do better, we must do better. I hope *Storying the Media World* contributes to the conversation of how that process might begin.

I am interested in the systemic underpinnings of communication within cultural studies. For students and scholars new to the field, or for journalists engaging with and hoping to learn from this book, it seems worthwhile to define a cultural studies approach to communication. As mass communication scholar Hanno Hardt writes: "A cultural studies approach leads to identifying and describing the means of communication, their social and material production, and their relations to other productive forces and to the social order in which they operate" (1988, 139). Though the examples from this book span 1991 through 2008, the notion that media can and must more fully represent everyday life has earlier roots in our field. In the words of Robert S. Alley: "Television can offer alternatives more consistent with humanistic values. It remains a slender reed, for were these series to suffer in the ratings, the result is predictable" (1985, 405). This book also pushes against the notion that communication can be easily solved or monetized, though profitability is an inevitable necessity for any business. Like mass communication scholars before me, I also bristle at the magic bullet myth, because I worry that it circumvents important conversations about media working toward deliberative democracy.

Describing the magic bullet myth, J. Michael Sproule notes that "the myth helped to suppress the implications for democratic life of modern communication practices" (1989, 226). Studying the cases presented in this book, I certainly benefit from Ott and Walter's understanding of Barthes's notion of intertextuality: "Since a text exists within an endlessly expanding matrix of intertextual production, readers continually bring new texts to bear upon their readings of that text" (2000, 431). I have worked, in the autoethnographic vignettes that open each chapter and indeed throughout the entire text, to be as transparent about how I am reading the texts studied as possible. I view this approach as in keeping with the broader critical and reflexive project of the work. In this way, I am certainly embracing Roger Stahl's formulation: "The very efficacy of the citizen in participatory democracy resides in a critical space that allows for public deliberation about important political matters" (2006, 125).

It should be said that most of the examples I have chosen are American and that several of them are related to American sports. Accordingly, my analysis is bolstered by existing understandings of the role of sports in American cultural life. As Michael L. Butterworth has perceptively articulated, "Sport is an enactment of American mythology, then, because it is driven by performance, the ability to conquer uncharted territory, and the prominence of individual acts of greatness" (2007, 232).

Finally, the notion of remembering, which is engaged personally and culturally in this book, is laden with normative consequences. As Sarah Florini writes: "Remembering is never an end in its own right, but a means of asserting power and legitimizing social relations" (2014, 315). As a media and memory scholar I recognize and appreciate the complicated, multifaceted work of remembering, especially its social and cultural impact. I have sought to directly engage that work in order to build toward a more diverse, pluralistic future for journalism and mass communication.

### The Plan for This Study

This volume contains this introduction and five chapters. In this introduction, I have articulated my purpose, provided necessary background, and anticipated the structure of my argument. In chapter 1 I use de Certeau's "narrated reality" (1988, 186) as a theoretical framework. Key terms are defined and historical, ethical, and philosophical underpinnings are provided. The analysis focuses on (1) how mediated narration too often uncritically elevates already powerful institutions; (2) how mediated narration tends to either not disturb or reinforce the existing power structure; and (3) how the implications of the actions prescribed in mediated narration most often have little, if any, potential to promote meaningful change. The critical exception to this rule is the case of the "Seven Days of Heroin" reportage by the staff of the *Cincinnati Enquirer*, which received the 2018 Pulitzer Prize for local reporting. I assert that this case indicates the need for a critical, poststructuralist turn in journalism.

In chapter 2 I use Stuart Hall's model of "operational fiction" (1974, 23) as a theoretical framework. The analysis reveals five operational fictions in this news reportage. The significance of each instance is decoded and the findings are contextualized. Application of critical theory explains the trouble with mediated narration as false completion, emphasizing the way that it fails to fully narrate the victims of the Sandy Hook shootings. My analysis calls for fuller narration, with clarity and respect, to help make sense of the lives and legacies of the victims. The chapter concludes with an examination of the process of storying new media technology history after Sandy Hook, underscoring the importance of naming the victims as part of retrospective coverage.

In chapter 3 I use Susan Wendell's (1989) feminist theory of disability as a theoretical framework, presenting a case narrative of found footage of FDR in a wheelchair that reveals an unnecessarily oppressive and reductive conception of the disabled body. I recognize critical theory as the seat of power through which to challenge the oppressive and reductive notion of the disability as something needing to be overcome. I admit that changing mediated narration surrounding the disabled body will likely require a generations-long and multifaceted effort, but considers this worthwhile and necessary work. The chapter concludes with calls for more pluralistic conceptions of what it means to be strong.

In chapter 4 I use Clifford Christians's concept of "authentic disclosure" (2007, 126) in news coverage as a theoretical framework in an assessment of the case of the *Cincinnati Enquirer*'s "Seven Days of Heroin" coverage, which received the 2018 Pulitzer Prize for local reporting. The findings highlight three themes in the reportage: (1) uncertainty from a sibling, (2) a call for help from a friend, and (3) a mother's grief. These themes emphasize that this reportage is rooted in the Christiansian call for historical, biographical news driven by lived experiences. The evidence in this case strongly suggests a model for storying the media world in a more diverse, pluralistic manner in the future.

In chapter 5 I bring together the theorists whose ideas are central to the book (de Certeau [1988]; Hall [1974]; Wendell [1989]; Christians [2007]), recognizing that each case studied in the book contains its own "complex culture" (Christians 2007, 126) that both needs and deserves fuller representation. A critical poststructuralist approach to journalism imbued with a Christiansian communitarian ethos shows itself well equipped both to story communities and to inform the public about the issues at the heart of those communities. I further consider a communitarian ethic as part of stewardship of and for the earth, inspired by the ideas of the poet and writer Wendell Berry (2013). With a Christiansian communitarian perspective, there does seem to be hope for a more pluralistic, diverse, humane, and, I hope, sustainable future for journalism and mass communication.

# 1   Storying the Media World

According to autoethnographers Ellis, Adams, and Bochner, "a researcher uses tenets of autobiography and ethnography to do and write autoethnography. Thus, as a method, autoethnography is both process and product" (2011, par. 1) I am storying myself into the media world, to provide a fuller understanding of the relationship between the self and the social in the media world. As Ellis, Adams, and Bochner explain: "When researchers do autoethnography, they retrospectively and selectively write about epiphanies that stem from, or are made possible by, being part of a culture and/or by possessing a particular cultural identity" (2011, par. 9). The epiphanies I have experienced amid mediated narration position me within this text. I begin with that admission as an invitation to the reader to join me in this book.

When I die I wish to be cremated. I do not have specific locations in mind where I wish my ashes to be scattered. There are so many geographies of personal importance to me, including college campuses, rivers, lakes, oceans, and even sports fields, that the task of where to scatter my ashes would likely include dozens, if not hundreds, of places. I do know this for sure: I would like the sports anthem "Charge!," the one often heard in stadiums, to be played at my remembrance ceremony. I want people to leave the ceremony inspired to live their passion(s), and I hope my lasting impact, as conveyed through this cheer, is to encourage people to live their lives to the very fullest. If this becomes my legacy, my life will have been well lived. Autoethnographer Art Bochner, grappling with the reality of Janice Hocker Rushing's death, stated: "I want to make sense of something that cannot be explained, only felt" (2006, 183). I articulate my own wish as a way to quell my fears of death. I story myself into the media world in hopes of guiding my legacy.

When humans are storied in the media world, we tend to hear most often about them from those already in power, including through official or governmental sources (see, for example, Gandy). There is a rhetorical pattern that emerges as a result: stories have a familiarity about them; we can identify them based on a series of specific markers that media scholars have noted as "news values" (see, most notably, Gans [2004]). Speaking as a critical-cultural scholar, I worry that consuming media sometimes means revisiting the same power brokers (local, state, national, international) for a retelling of very similar narratives (see, for example, Hall). This worry has its roots in an autoethnographic (see, for example, Ellis [1999]) bind for me. As a person with cerebral palsy, I must be vulnerable enough (see, for example, Gloviczki [2015]) to admit that I do not predictably see myself (or anyone like me) in the daily news cycle. For all of my considerable privilege—I am white, male, employed, and tenured on the tenure track in my degree field, healthy, heterosexual, educated—I am also unimpeachably different because of my physical disability. I join others who have written about difference in similar ways (see, for example, Pate [2011]). Like autoethnographer Sarah Wall, I realize "difficulties . . . emerge from such a complex intersection of social locations." (2008, 40). I am both invigorated and daunted by all these identities.

Balancing difference and privilege has called me to initiate this study. In my first book, *Journalism and Memorialization in the Age of Social Media*, I included a consideration of legacy construction in the aftermath of the 2007 Virginia Tech school shootings. In this second book I not only consider the Sandy Hook shootings in Newtown, Connecticut, but I also present a call for a more thorough, multivocal journalism within and beyond the coverage of school shootings. Rethinking journalism, telling more stories about victims and fewer about shooters and emphasizing narratives instead of easily visualizable components, is also to rethink who we wish to remember and how we wish to remember them. Embracing the importance of reflexive vulnerability (see, for example, Richardson [2007]), I open this book with an autoethnographic vignette about how I wish to be remembered. The fictional movie *Draft Day* features a scene in which Sonny Weaver Sr., former coach of the National Football League's (NFL) Cleveland Browns, wishes to have his ashes scattered on the 50-yard line of a practice field named in his honor. Using autoethnography as a methodological lens to examine this scene, I realize that it has inspired my thinking about my own final wishes. Just as autoethnographer Mariza Méndez has done, I am exploring autoethnographically "to contribute to others' lives by making them reflect on and empathise with the narratives presented." (2014, 282).

Moreover, this realization sparks my thinking about how popular culture, including fictionalized accounts, can influence real world decision-making. Death is one season of life, and individuals have the opportunity, and perhaps the responsibility, to convey their final wishes to those people who potentially have power to make the wishes come true. As I have written in the past, football is a valuable part of my identity. The story of the scene fits nicely into a narrative of the game as cultural force, important enough to certain people that they wish to have their ashes scattered on the field. After I read autoethnographer Carolyn Ellis's "Grave Tending: With Mom at the Cemetery" (2006), I became motivated to examine my own perspectives on remembrance in a family context. Autoethnographer Arthur Bochner's work has also encouraged me to clarify my own wishes. I am especially thinking about Bochner's assertion: "Death can arrive at any moment. Medical research is finding remedies for more and more illnesses, but no cure exists for the impermanence of life" (2006, 184). I choose to embrace Bochner's words, focusing on what life is and can be.

One year I begged my parents for a Mickey Mantle autograph. I wanted a ball in the hand of The Mick. They granted my wish, and I received the ball with Mickey's signature. Years later I learned the ball was actually a fake (see "Operation Bullpen"). The Mick never signed it. My parents didn't know either. They bought a baseball that had been one among many in a nationwide autograph scam. Mickey Mantle is dead: the proximity I had to him through the ball is gone, too. I am grateful, though, for my Mantle story. The memory of receiving the ball is alive in me. The way the trinkets I gathered reminded me of my heroes, how I used sports to understand the pace of the body. When one grows up with a disability, the body becomes (and presents) a challenge. The Mick and other heroes were unknowing liberators of mine. I saw in their physical prowess the potential that was just out of my reach and yet toward which I was striving. So it is not the Mick himself, flawed as he was, or the ball I received, flawed as it was, that mattered. Mickey Mantle is dead, but the impact of the ball is the story that unfolded in me. The ball feels good today as a gift, its goodness having been transformed away from its association with the Mick. Making that emotional journey was an iterative process, though, because I had to learn to appreciate the ball in a different way.

Self-awareness comes slowly to a young boy unafraid to swing and miss. I clung to the dream of being a professional baseball player for quite a long time. I was always ready with Jim Abbott as an example. Though he is not disabled in the way that I am, I saw in Abbott the potential for difference on the field. And when you're young, with or without a disability, all you want to be is normal. So I picked other sports heroes. First, Joe Montana; then Kirby Puckett; and later Tom Glavine, Kevin Garnett, Shaquille O'Neal, and Mickey Mantle, among a host of others. Images of them in action made their way into my bedroom. In the way that young boys use what space they have to build shrines, I remember my posters. My boyish castle was a study in contrasts: I had a room full of athletes and their superhuman abilities, while I was unable to tie my own shoes or zip up my winter coat. Against the backdrop of relative absence, presence overwhelms. When I was thirsty, I drank from the water fountain at school for as many seconds as I could.

And yet I was fairly active in sports to the extent that I could be. I played every game the others did—baseball, basketball, T-ball, kickball—shot the ball into the hoop in our driveway. When I got tired I sat down or called myself out for a bit. I hated limits, was mad to admit I had any, and yet knew I sometimes had no choice. Reliving the story of my boyhood culture, I followed autoethnographer Sarah Wall in that "I relied on the memories of my lived experience" (2008, 45). The boundaries on the playing field existed alongside the limits my body presented amidst play. I wondered, even from a young age, why play was so much work. Accordingly, I was probably interacting with the corporeal realities of my body from a young age. Striking the baseball off the tee on one occasion, I remember being distinctly surprised at how far the ball had traveled. I had to learn my limits before I learned to transcend them.

Like autoethnographers before me (see, for example, Holman Jones [2013]; Wyatt[2013]; Gingrich-Philbrook [2013]), I think about how thresholds signify, and celebrate, transmission from one psychic space to another. My body will tire of walking at some point. I also feel a sense of sadness at the inevitability of this age-related shift in my life. I have got thirty-one years, I hope, of ambulatory life left (and-fingers-and-toes-crossed-for-more) but I am beginning to feel the weight of that clock. My worry is that life seated will skew my vantage points, which is perhaps a vain worry and one that I carry with a twinge of shame in my heart.

Having worked with disabled students in the past, I can safely say that they have taught me considerably more than I have ever taught them. About fortitude, persistence. Ignoring the impressions of others. Setting and achieving goals. And yet in becoming wheelchair bound I know I will be othering myself in a way that feels uncomfortable to me. So I write this book as a coping strategy, a preemptive way to lean into my discomfort. I also with a bit of humor welcome the fact that in a wheelchair I will not sweat as much as I do on my feet, always looking for the silver lining in what I otherwise perceive (perhaps wrongly) as an oncoming cloud. As autoethnographer Keith Berry persuasively articulates: "Writing cultural accounts, like interacting with a trusted comrade, can and should feel intimate, imaginative, and dialogic" (2006, par. 3). I draw the reader into the lifeworld of my worries in the above paragraph in the hope of building that sense of intimacy.

About a year ago I attended a celebration of life for one of the gentleman who lived in my mother's building. He lived a long, seemingly happy and productive life. At the celebration we were out on a balcony with the Mississippi River in the distance. The family asked me to take a picture for them, and I, of course, did. But there was nothing to hang on to while I steadied the iPhone to get the family members all into the shot, and I felt myself becoming unsteady. My mom stood behind me to steady me and to give me someone to lean back onto, and I took the picture for the family. I have stood on my own two feet to take pictures in the past, , but this time, for whatever reason, it was not to be. In this instance I felt the body in an adversarial exchange with me, reminding me of what might be in store, the potential for a nonambulatory future.

And then there is this: I was asked "who drives me" during an eye consultation recently, as though someone must, a reminder mostly I think of the dominance of car culture in the Western world. I write into/toward an emancipatory threshold where Elon Musk or some such inventor succeeds in a technology that drives me. My body will need more help as it gets older, but getting older is a gift I am working, and struggling, to embrace. I write in hopes of smoothing, and soothing, that struggle. I imagine that my affinity for water emerges because the water is a liberatory space for my body. For example, the jumping that is nearly impossible for me on land becomes doable in water. Following autoethnographer Joshua Pate, "I strive for others to avoid making my physical capabilities my only means of identification" (2011, 3–4); but it is true that water extends my body and so I work to immerse myself in it whenever I can. Immersion seems a fitting response in a city like Minneapolis, known for its water. As I have written about in the past, water (see, for example, Gloviczki [2020]), especially in Minneapolis, affords me a spiritual sense of hope and of home.

When I was a sophomore in college I traveled to Prague for a January term course. While there I was required to keep a course journal and so I wrote almost every day, usually in the mornings or before bed at night, cataloging what we did that day and to a lesser extent how our work made me feel. This is the first time I remember prolonged, daily writing, though I certainly jotted poems and kept a (very occasional) diary as a young child. Articulating the connections in this autoethnographic vignette provides me "opportunities to define disability, rather than allowing disability to define the individual" (Pate 2011, 14). Following cultural theorist Michel de Certeau, I believe that "every story is a travel story—a spatial practice," (1988, 115), and I feel fortunate that my journey continues to reveal one locale, then the next, that serves to fuse them together across my life's narrative, embracing an around-the-world geography.

## Making Sense of Narrated Reality

The purpose of this chapter is to present a de Certeauean narrated reality analysis of the case of a new media technology history of mediated bodies (1991–2018). De Certeau's conception of narrated reality is the most appropriate theoretical lens for this chapter because it focuses on mediated narration as a normative act, one that shapes how audiences make sense of content and context. De Certeau asserts that "narrated reality constantly tells us what must be believed and what must be done" (1988, 186). The core element of narrated reality is that media promote an understanding of power relations insulated from critique: what is narrated as powerful is what is powerful. Mediated narration first captures faith ("what must be believed"), then prescribes action ("what must be done"). The core of narrated reality is especially instructive when the content being narrated is unbelievable or unusual.

Invoking the journey from faith to action, de Certeau asserts media provide a way of knowing the world. The use of this theory in this chapter is instructive in three ways: (1) to understand the characteristics mediated narration tends to elevate as worthy of audience members' faith ("what must be believed"); (2) to understand the actions mediated narration tends to prescribe for audience members ("what must be done"); and (3) to understand how the narration may prescribe certain actions for social change.

Following Berger and Luckmann, I "define 'reality' as a quality appertaining to phenomena that we recognize as having a being independent of our own volition" (1967, 1). I am especially interested in how new media influence the realities of its audience(s). To this end, I employ Neil Postman's perception: "Without a medium to create its form, the news of the day does not exist" (1985, 8). Braiding Berger and Luckmann into Postman, I recognize that mediated realities are often influenced by the content produced within them. Though media and mediation are certainly just one part of any individual's broader reality, I do assert that mediated representations may influence what individuals know (or what they think they know) about topics being mediated. I invoke Stuart Hall on ideology to underscore that point. As Hall writes: "the media's main sphere of operations is the production and transformation of ideologies" (1995, 18). I specifically assert that, when audiences have limited knowledge about a given topic, mediated representations may provide an especially persuasive source of information about that topic.

### What Is Critical?

Following Ott and Mack: "Critical media studies is an umbrella term used to describe an array of theoretical perspectives which, though diverse, are united by their skeptical attitude, humanistic approach, political assessment, and commitment to social justice." (2013, 15)

### What Is Poststructuralism?

Following Davies and Gannon: "Through analysis of texts and talk, it [poststructuralism] shows how relations of power are constructed and maintained by granting normality, rationality and naturalness to the dominant term in any binary, and in contrast, how the subordinated term is marked as other, as lacking, as not ratio-nal." (2012, 312)

**What Is the News Environment?**
Following Hermida: "The news is a constant buzz in the back-ground, available at any time, on any device, in just about any place, and is produced by both professionals and the audience it-self." (2016, 3)

It is my hope that these key terms will help students and scholars more fully make sense of what follows in the chapter and the book. In addi-tion to the cases studied, *Storying the Media World* has historical, ethi-cal, and philosophical underpinnings in the writings of sportswriter Bob Considine, the communitarianism of media ethicist Clifford Christians, and the existentialism of philosopher Albert Camus respectively.

The American sportswriters of the 1930s were certainly on the right track in reportage that foregrounded the body. Consider the following example from Bob Considine: "Listen to this, buddy, for it comes from a guy whose palms are still wet, whose throat is still dry, and whose jaw is still agape from the utter shock of watching Joe Louis knock out Max Schmeling" (1999, 138). So begins one of the exemplars in David Halberstam's iconic anthology *The Best American Sportswriting of the Century*. I wish to focus on the descriptive call in the excerpt, the invi-tation to the reader to notice how the journalist's body has been influ-enced (indeed altered) by the experience of witnessing the event in per-son and now sharing that description with the audience. The journalist here displays vulnerability: invoking his own body decenters the notion of the journalist as all-knowing observer. The detached, authoritative ac-count becomes more subjective, even evocative in its telling. The decla-ration "Listen to this, buddy," reminds one of the way a best friend leans in to whisper a treasured secret to another: a term of endearment, espe-cially between men. The subsequent description—"for it comes from a guy whose palms are still wet, whose throat is still dry, and whose jaw is still agape from the utter shock of watching Joe Louis knock out Max Schmeling"—reveals Considine sharing with the audience the body's au-thority to share this story. In other words, this passage reveals a prom-ise: just as Considine's body has been affected, so too might the audience be affected. When Considine opens this column, he draws the reader in by beginning with himself. The journalist begins with his own experience. In doing so Considine showcases the first-person appeal as a journalistic device. In this example from 1938, the journalist emphasizes the visceral present of reporting. Beginning with the self invites the other. Evocative, direct language welcomes the reader into the community being described. The body provides a shared text from which to begin the experience of sending, receiving, and making sense of media content.

Authentic disclosure about the ways journalists are experiencing the visceral present today can more robustly foreground previously underreported narratives. A shift in mediated narration requires consideration of what Considine produced on the page in 1938 and recognition of the fact that he was a mediated being who was writing in and through a mediated body. The tools of the trade have evolved in the last eighty years, and I argue that journalism should harness that evolution while retaining and returning to the heart of its narratives, with a focus on people, their histories, and their stories.

Following media ethicist Clifford Christians, I advocate turning away from a utilitarian approach to ethics and toward a dialogic perspective. As Christians writes: "A more sophisticated concept of news, consistent with dialogical ethics, is authentic disclosure. In this perspective, reporting must be grounded historically and biographically, so that complex cultures are represented adequately" (2007, 126). Specifically, I endorse a Christiansian communitarian perspective, in which "we are born into a sociocultural universe where values, moral commitments, and existential meanings are negotiated dialogically" (124). I read in Christians's words an opportunity to work toward reconceptualization of the media world. In Christians's work as a media ethicist, I have found the systems of thought that he begins from to be particularly instructive for their breadth. Christians looks broad and deep for the underpinnings of the ethical world. In this call for fuller representation, I am reading a deep ethical calling as well. His words suggest that fuller representation is how the world ought to be. I agree with him and so happily carry forward that call. It is my hope that theoretical insights from the past continue to inform not only our scholarly understanding(s) of new media technology history but that such insights will also help show the path that we as media, technology, and society scholars chart forward together into the future.

In philosophical terms, in this chapter and throughout this inquiry I take the position that mediated bodies are storied through youth to death with a sense of existential vanity: the body only matters as long as it is an instrument through and for audience adoration. Albert Camus's "Summer in Algiers" (2018) provides the philosophical underpinnings for this perspective. Camus writes about the way that the body is both liberated in Algiers and also forever fated toward gradual decline. The corporeal formation articulated in "Summer in Algiers" celebrates youth and bemoans elder years in a way similar to that of American media consumer culture. As Camus asserts: "During their entire youth men find here a life in proportion to their beauty. Then, later on, the downhill slope and obscurity. They wagered on flesh, but knowing they were to lose" (142).

Camus is primarily concerned with the decline of the body through the progression from youth to old age, recognizing that all bodies will cease to exist and indeed all lives will end. He considers this transformation (birth-death) to be an inevitable aspect of existence. For Camus, the body both reflects and reinforces this process. Amid this existential reality, Camus emphasizes the way it becomes necessary to celebrate the body, to make space for it, as it exists in the spatial-temporal present.

Writing in a postwar context, the grim shadow of conflict etched into the authorial landscape. In this environment, the moment becomes the order of the day. To recognize the moment is also to recognize that any moment is necessarily fleeting. Time exists to mark human passage from youth into eventual death. The body is the hub within which, and through which, life is lived. It constitutes evidence of and the vehicle for existence. Our bodies are how and why we participate in the human experience. For Camus, the body is also often place bound. Hence the letter to Algiers and its elevation in analysis, separating it from "old walled towns like Paris, Prague, and even Florence" (2018, 141). Camus recognizes that where a body exists, its geographic and structural landscape, carries with it certain affordances and constraints. Bodies benefit from space that allows them to be fully expressed. In this chapter I interrogate how, why, and where bodies are located amid mediated narration, as well as where bodies are not, and the impact of that absence. To omit mention of the body is to level all bodies as able-bodied, capable and even heroic in similar ways. In other words, to cover the body in what amounts to largely an athletic, heroic manner is to erase bodies that do not or cannot rise to that standard.

Robert E. Stake's (1994) collective case study provides the methodological toolkit for this chapter. The methodology emphasizes that instrumental cases "are chosen because it is believed that understanding them will lead to better understanding, perhaps better theorizing, about a still larger collection of cases" (237). Focused on a twenty-seven-year period (1991–2018), I investigate seven cases to chart the history and development of new media technology within the context of mediated narration. As more media coverage appears online, particularly through video platforms such as YouTube, the tools to produce and disseminate news are widely available and actively consumed. While individuals have more power than ever to tell their own stories, using their own tools in their own voices, these cases reveal mediated narration most often reinforces existing power dynamics instead of giving voice to the pluralistic, diverse communities yearning for and worthy of fuller representation.

Accordingly, I propose that the underlying lesson of these cases is for journalists and audiences to employ digital media tools in their production and consumption of media content in order to more fully advocate for underrepresented populations. Specifically, the cases reveal that (1) mediated narration most often uncritically elevates the characteristics that have made the individuals or institutions powerful as justification for why they "must be believed" (de Certeau 1988, 186), (2) mediated narration tends to prescribe actions for audience members that either do not disturb the existing power structure or serve to reinforce the existing power structure ("what must be done") (de Certeau 1988, 186), and (3) the implications of the prescribed actions most often have little, if any, potential to promote meaningful social change.

The critical exception to this rule is the case of the "Seven Days of Heroin" reportage by the staff of the *Cincinnati Enquirer*, which received the 2018 Pulitzer Prize for local reporting. I assert that this case, the seventh and final case presented in the chapter, indicates the need for a critical, poststructuralist turn in journalism, to foreground histories, biographies, and lived experiences. "Seven Days of Heroin" strongly suggests that digital media production and consumption have untapped potential. Taking this case as exemplar, the process of storying the media world can more holistically represent the ways individuals and institutions engage with one another during times of crisis and throughout everyday life. I conclude the findings section with the assertion that

"Seven Days of Heroin" provides a model for the future of journalism and mass communication.

## Overview of Each of the Case Studies

As a collective case study, this chapter contains seven case studies (Stake 1994, 237). In this section of chapter 1, I provide an overview of each of the case studies. I have elected to organize the case studies in chronological order, because the growth and development of technology across the time period studied in this chapter (1991–2018) is vital to understanding this chapter as a new media technology history. This chapter opens during a methodological moment in communication and related fields in which "a blurring of disciplinary boundaries has occurred" (Stake 1994, xi).

I certainly benefit from this moment as a case study researcher because such disciplinary blurring focuses attention on the case itself, more or less regardless of where each case may find its disciplinary home. Disciplinary blurring arguably helps bring each case into focus. As Stake articulates: "With its own unique history, the case is a complex entity operating within a number of contexts, including the physical, economic, ethical and aesthetic" (1994, 239). In this chapter, I focus on how each case employs de Certeau's narrated reality to reinforce and strengthen the power dynamic at the core of its storytelling. As de Certeau writes: "From morning to night, narrations constantly haunt streets and buildings. They articulate our existences by teaching us what they must be. They 'cover the event,' that is to say, they *make* our legends (*legenda*, what is to be read and said) out of it" (1988, 186, emphasis in original). In this chapter I begin from the underlying assumption that each case is imbued with a de Certeauean legend to structure its power dynamic. Studying mediated narration allows me to point to, critique, and make sense of the power dynamic in each case.

### 1. Gene Larkin's Pinch Hit in the World Series (1991)

"Minnesota bench. Hoping to get this winning run across here in the tenth. It's carried by Dan Gladden at third. Bases loaded, one out. Infielders are sort of halfway at second and short. Pena in a jam." [Larkin makes contact with the ball, which eventually falls into the gap in left center field.] Broadcaster: "The Twins are gonna win the World Series.

The Twins have won it. It's a base hit. It's a one–nothing, ten-inning victory." [Twins players cheering as they rush the field. Metrodome crowd ecstatic.] (Overheard among Twins players: "what a game") [Braves players appear deflated]. Broadcaster: "With the outfield in, the high fastball from Alejandro Pena to Gene Larkin" [Replay of base hit] ("1999 WS Gm7" 2013, 00:00–00:01:43).

*2. Mickey Mantle's Funeral (1995)*
"Mickey Mantle was an American dream come to life. Today, teammates and fans bid him a final farewell" (Rather and Mabry 1995, 00:00:00–00:01:40; the 18-word passage quoted here represents the key passage in a 230-word news report).

*3. The Celtic FC Fan in Soccer Shrines (2010)*
"I was born about ten minutes from Celtic Park. And now forty-one years later, I'm still here, ten minutes from the stadium. It's match day today, so now I'm getting ready to go to the game. I'm really lucky, I work at Celtic Park. So for me, the whole match day experience starts the minute I get out of bed in the morning. Every match is so important. Every match is [inaudible] to win, need to win. I'm never gonna play for Celtic, so for me this is the next best thing: putting on these green and white hoops. And being part of the team, and going to the match" ("Soccer Shrines Glasgow" 2018, 00:01:43–00:02:20).

*4. The Shooting at Sandy Hook in Newtown, Connecticut (2012)*
"Lanza entered the building, carrying a Bushmaster AR-15 assault rifle, with two semi-automatic handguns inside the pockets of his military style cargo pants" ("Newtown Massacre" 2012, 0:00:00–0:02:37; the twenty-three-word passage quoted here represents the key passage in a 430-word news report).

*5. Franklin Delano Roosevelt Found Footage (2013)*
"Being pushed in a wheelchair" ("Myth of Roosevelt's Wheelchair" 2013, 0:00:00–0:00:23; the five-word passage quoted here represents the key phrase in a sixty-nine-word news report).

*6. Sonny Weaver Sr.'s Body in* Draft Day *(2014)*

*Sonny Weaver Jr.* You want to spread these goddamn ashes, you do it tomorrow.

Mrs. Barb Weaver (widow) No.

Sonny Weaver Jr. I'm serious.

Mrs. Barb Weaver (widow) No! Now then, are you going to read this prayer as your father asked you to?

Sonny Weaver Jr. No, I'm not. Not today.

Mrs. Barb Weaver (widow) I'll do it myself.

Uncredited Woman in Office (to Ali) Good luck.

Ali to Sonny: How 'bout some fresh air?

Sonny Weaver Jr.: Whoever thought it meant that much to him? Naming a simple practice field in his honor. God, he took pride in the weirdest things.

Ali: He was your father, Sonny. What was it, why did you hate him so much?

Sonny Weaver Jr. I didn't hate my father. You know what, everyone always gives me grief for firing my father.

Ali: Well, you did. I was here that day.

Sonny Weaver Jr. It was my mother.

Ali: What?

Sonny Weaver Jr. It was my moth . . . look don't get me wrong, I'm the one who fired him, but it was my mother who asked me to do it. My dad's doctors told him that the stress of coaching was gonna kill him, so . . . of course, he refused to retire. So now I have a choice. The time he has left at home with my mother. Or another year on the another year on the sidelines where maybe he drops dead on national television. So what do you do? I gave it to my mom, and I fired him.

Ali: How come you never told me that before?

Sonny Weaver Jr.: You know, there's already so many versions of what happened that it's not really something I love talking about.

Ali: You never told him . . . You j-just. You let him believe that his only son would just fire him.

Sonny Weaver Jr.: That's how we do things in my family . . .

Ali: Sonny . . .

Sonny Weaver Jr.: You know, all I ever wanted to do was just get him a ring. Ah jeez, what is this?

Ali: They want to pay their respects. (Draft Day 2014, 0:00:00–0:02:41).

*7. The* Cincinnati Enquirer's *"Seven Days of Heroin" Reportage (2017)*

"Babies will be born to heroin addicted mothers. Courts will take children from addicted parents. Taxpayers will spend heavily to lock up drug users. People will overdose in gas stations and parks and school parking lots. It's the first day of another week of the heroin epidemic. Over the next seven days in greater Cincinnati, at least 180 people will overdose. Eighteen will die. This is normal now. This is a typical week. Here's courtroom A in Hamilton County. It's the first stop for those arrested the night before on heroin charges. On this morning, as on most, one in four cases on the docket is directly connected to heroin. They come from wealthy neighborhoods and poor, they are young and old, parents and grandparents, sons and daughters. Sometimes, they are brought here hours after they almost died from an overdose. Sometimes, they don't make it to court. Heroin and other opiates kill one American every sixteen minutes. That's more than die in traffic crashes."

> [1:45 p.m., Monday, July 10]
> "Cincinnati 911, what is the address of your emergency?"
> "4980 Glenway Avenue, the Covedale Library. My children's librarian is asking for Narcan. She thinks that he may be overdosing" (Cincinnati.com 2017, 0:00:00–0:02:12).

## Lessons from Each Case Study

Each of the seven case studies reveals meaningful lessons. I present them below in chronological order:

**1. Gene Larkin's Pinch Hit in the World Series (1991)** On October 27, 1991, pinch hitter Gene Larkin struck a tenth inning base hit into the gap in left-center field to win the World Series for the Minnesota Twins. In *The Practice of Everyday Life*, cultural theorist Michel de Certeau asserts: "Narrated reality constantly tells us what must be believed and what must be done" (1988, 186). Journalism as a social practice constructs what happened, as well as often how it happened, and sometimes why it happened, in its storytelling. The call to action in the Larkin footage is for the audience to celebrate: the underdog team has defeated the favorite in nail-biting fashion.

As a case within new media technology history, Major League Baseball has ostensibly uploaded this moment to emphasize the enduring appeal of David defeating Goliath in American culture. Storying Larkin's hit in this manner places this story into an easily understandable narrative framework: the crafty athlete has used his talents to emerge victorious. This reportage reveals the reductive quality of mediated narration into an oversimplified binary structure: the nonstar athlete employs tools usually reserved for the star athlete to capture a win for his team. Larkin's heroic act is reinforced as a rare instance because the position of the media star must be protected and in this case is protected, in and through mediated narration. The reportage strongly suggests that the audience can cheer Larkin's act because he has acted as a star would have acted. Larkin's body is an allusion toward enduring possibility.

Leading into a pivotal moment in the seventh (and final) game of the 1991 World Series, the broadcaster sets the scene for the audience with the following words: "The Minnesota bench hoping to get this winning run across here in the tenth. It's carried by Dan Gladden at third. Bases loaded, one out. Infielders are sort of halfway at second and short[stop]. Pena in a jam. [Larkin swings, makes contact with the ball and sends it into the gap in left-center field]. The Twins are gonna win the World Series. The Twins have won it. It's a base hit. It's a 1–0 ten-inning victory" ("1991 WS Gm7" 2013, 0:00:00–0:00:31). The unlikely sports hero, in this instance Larkin, is an unacknowledged body. Most notable in the narration of Larkin's at bat is that his name is mentioned only once in the entire video clip, as the last two words of it. His body needs not be acknowledged, following de Certeau (1988), because it only has meaning in relationship to the runner on third base (Dan Gladden, who is only meaningful in this context because he represents the winning run).

The unlikely sports hero thus blends (or blurs) into the team, as an instrument that gives rise to the team's success. This emphasis on the team is reinforced in the narration: First "the Minnesota bench"; second "the Twins are gonna win"; and third "the Twins have won." In this way, the news narration tightly wraps up the central story in an easily recognizable, even timeless, form of storytelling: there was a past (while the team watched and waited), there is a present (the team winning), and there will be a future (the team as baseball's 1991 World Series champions). In the Larkin case, the rise of the nonstar athlete is understood through the lens of the star athlete. The power dynamic is undisturbed, fully intact. Larkin is the nonstar athlete who for a moment wore the cloak of the star athlete. Thus, the reportage reinforces the existing structure: Larkin's act is as an athlete standing in—quite literally pinch hitting—for a star. Neither the journalist nor the audience need worry about the lens of the "star athlete" because Larkin is simply standing in for a star in this case. No other social action by any party is required or requested. To make such an invocation would be to challenge the dominant power structure, and the reportage does not appear to want to broach that possibility. The pinch hitter has the potential to challenge a star's power, so the pinch hitter is not focused upon, in order to protect the star's power.

**2. Mickey Mantle's Funeral (1995)** On August 15, 1995, CBS *Evening News* anchor Dan Rather reported on the funeral for New York Yankees player Mickey Mantle. "Mickey Mantle was an American dream come to life," Rather said. "Today, teammates and fans bid him a final farewell" (Rather and Mabry 1995, 5:56:30–5:56:37). The bona fide sports hero, in this instance Mantle, is an aspirational body. Mantle's death is narrated as an American loss because Mantle was, in Rather's words, "an American dream come to life." Rather's reportage about Mantle offers an aspirational narrative to the audience, one that is ultimately unobtainable because the hero has passed away.

Represented through language ("the American dream") as the real that was also ideal, Mantle is equated in this reportage with all that is desirable in our culture. Mantle's loss is not only his own; all who aspire to the American dream are drawn into the loss, Rather's language suggests, through our shared aspiration. Reading de Certeau's (1988) theory about the bridge from faith to action while examining broadcast television news offers a prescription: Mantle was a hero, he has died, and now we, the audience, should remember him. Whether or not this prescription represents any kind of comfort for the audience, the gravity of the event, as presented, does suggest that a coping mechanism may be useful and remembrance is suggested as a strategy. Put another way, the news narrative itself—remembrance earned because of his rise and put into practice after his fall—is presented as a coping mechanism in the aftermath of tragedy.

Television coverage of Mantle's funeral suggests the power of a news narrative to reinforce and strengthen existing hierarchical structures in mainstream culture. The social action suggested by reportage (remembrance) serves only to reinforce the dominant memory of Mantle. The one option that is presented to the audience—to remember Mantle as a hero—will not lead to any social change. Remembrance in this manner only serves to reinforce and strengthen the existing power dynamic.

3. The Celtic FC Fan in *Soccer Shrines* (2010) Whereas Mantle was celebrated as the ideal athlete, the spectator's body is celebrated for its proximity to the ideal athlete. As the television program *Soccer Shrines* reveals in its 2010 profile of a Celtic soccer (football) fan: "I was born about ten minutes from Celtic Park. And now forty-one years later, I'm still here, ten minutes from the stadium. It's match day today, so now I'm getting ready to go to the game. I'm really lucky, I work at Celtic Park. So for me, the whole match day experience starts the minute I get out of bed in the morning. Every match is so important. Every match is [inaudible] to win, need to win. I'm never gonna play for Celtic, so for me this is the next best thing: putting on these green and white hoops. And being part of the team, and going to the match" ("Soccer Shrines" 2010, 00:01:43–00:02:20).

The sports fan, in the instance of *Soccer Shrines*, is a body made visible for/through proximity. Spectatorship thus becomes a certain kind of membership for the sports fan featured in this segment of the documentary. Blending his reality with that of the team, in such a way that it is difficult to recognize where one stops and the other begins, media's shaping of culture resonates throughout this example. The sports fan featured in this segment narrates his reality of getting dressed in the team's iconic color bands as being "part of the team." Storying his day within the lifeworld of the team's day ("match day"), he has both written himself into the story of the team and reinforced that story.

More importantly, though, the fan has also authored a third way: the individual fan as an exemplar of and for the team. His body is represented as most valuable, in fact, when it is present near the team, at the game, inside the stadium: the body as proximal "part of the team." Representing and constructing the sports fan, as *Soccer Shrines* does in this example, embodies the belief in the role of the audience as part of the team that is popularized in Western culture.

Such examples confer an emotive experience as well, the psychic benefit of almost-team membership from a distance, especially if the fan in question is decked out in the team gear (the team kit) or has elements of paraphernalia (jerseys, hats, scarves) that promote identification with the experience of sports fandom. Spectators recognize and embrace their proximity as I did when watching Larkin as a young child. Proximity to their team is how they profess what they "believe" in de Certeauean narrated reality terms, and elation for their team's victory is what they "do." Faith and action have been taught to fans through the narrated reality of other fans across their mediated experiences. Proximity to the team is a lie by the journalist and a lie to the audience, because no amount of costuming will effectively allow the fan to help the team to victory. Cheering is ultimately unlikely to influence the team's performance. Little if any meaningful social action will result owing to fandom.

**4. The Shooting at Sandy Hook in Newtown, Connecticut (2012)** On December 14, 2012, twenty-eight people were killed and two were injured in the Sandy Hook school shooting in Newtown. In *The Practice of Everyday Life*, de Certeau argues: "The weak must continually turn to their own ends forces alien to them" (1988, xix). Journalism as a social practice constructs dynamics between those individuals who possess power and those who are in need of power. The call to action in the Sandy Hook footage is to recognize the irrefutable power of firearms, especially as tools of the powerful to murder the powerless.

As a case within new media technology history, CBS News ostensibly uses a video time line to shed light on the most easily visualizable elements of this tragedy. Storying Sandy Hook in this manner places this story into an easily understandable narrative framework: the use of guns has ended human life. This reportage oversimplifies Sandy Hook as the story of a murderer and his murders, minimizing the victims and their legacies. For example, two headshots (one of Adam Lanza and one of his mother) are prominently featured as part of the mediated narration. The inclusion of these headshots is significant because a headshot is a representational ghost. The body is implied but never actually seen. Thus its power is reinforced as it is unable even to face any challenge. The most important image from this nineteen seconds of footage is arguably when the headshots of Lanza and his mother are placed side-by-side on screen.

In the Sandy Hook case, the death of the victims is understood through the violent act of the shooter and, specifically, through his use of firearms to commit murder. The shooter's tools, his preparation, and his operationalization of his plan are highlighted in the reportage to justify how he committed these atrocities. The Sandy Hook reportage is meant to story how the victims died, rather than how they lived. At Sandy Hook the weak are overpowered by the shooter, so they cannot do anything to "turn [the situation] to their own ends" (de Certeau 1988, xix; brackets mine).

Amid tragedy the core elements of narrated reality, the journey from faith to action, are again prominent in the Sandy Hook shooting. The victims' deaths are "believed" (faith) and no action is suggested because ostensibly nothing can overcome high-powered weapons. In other words, "what is to be done" (action) is answered via absence: nothing can be done. In de Certeauean terms, focusing the reportage on Lanza effectively absolves both the journalist and the audience from the need to take bona fide action. His plan was too sophisticated, his weapons were too powerful. Though they are not mentioned outright, it is reasonable to suggest (based on the history of the last twenty years of school shootings in America) that prayers should be given, but prayers are arguably unlikely to bring about meaningful social change. Put simply, even if prayer had been invoked (as it often has been), change is unlikely to be the result of prayer, because guns are too powerful.

5. **Franklin Delano Roosevelt Found Footage (2013)** On July 10, 2013, CBS News uploaded a video to their YouTube channel featuring former U.S. president Franklin Delano Roosevelt "being pushed" in a wheelchair. As de Certeau writes: "From morning to night, narrations consistently haunt streets and buildings. They articulate our existences by teaching us what they must be. They 'cover the event,' that is to say, they *make* our legends (*legenda*, what is to be read and said) out of it" (1988, 186; emphasis in original). Journalism as a social practice constructs heroes, often by shining a light on their heroism.

The call to action in the video footage is to reflect and reinforce Roosevelt's relatively rare status in the visible social order of the day, as a politician who was also a disabled person. As a case within new media technology history, CBS *This Morning*'s storytelling emphasizes what Roosevelt cannot do, owing to his disability, thus framing disability as impossibility rather than possibility. Storying Roosevelt's wheelchair footage in this manner emphasizes that disabled individuals can overcome physical limitations in instances of exceptional power, grace, and charisma.

This reportage oversimplifies the disabled experience as one that foregrounds challenges rather than opportunities for meaningful living. Roosevelt's body is "being pushed" passively out of view, the body itself is ostensibly invisible, meaningful largely for its eventual erasure from the scene through the use of an unrelated remark by the journalist. Journalist Gayle King reported: "More than six decades after his death, we're getting our very first look at President Franklin Roosevelt being pushed in a wheelchair. This is an interesting story because it's something that the public never saw throughout his life. This film only eight seconds long was found in the National Archives by a professor from Franklin College, which by the way, was actually named for Benjamin Franklin, and not FDR" ("Myth of FDR's Wheelchair" 2013, 0:00:00–0:00:24).

The disabled person, in this instance Roosevelt, is an invisible body. Roosevelt's body is notable for its "being pushed," thus removing any agency from his body and placing the power with the individual who is doing the pushing. Because the wheelchair pusher is unnamed, it is as though the body is floating through the ether, "being pushed" rather than Roosevelt (or anyone else for that matter) pushing it. It is hard to escape the notion of a body "being pushed" as a ghost body.

The news narration in this instance also diminishes any possibilities of meaningful consideration about a disabled body, by ending the news item with information about Franklin College. Whether or not this information was intended as a joke, its relatively unrelated quality to FDR "being pushed," serves to soften the overall seriousness of the story, thus reinforcing the invisibility of the disabled body. In the Roosevelt case, his disability is narrated as a rare attribute of a powerful politician. Emphasizing in the reportage how Roosevelt was rarely represented as disabled in the public eye reinforces the strangeness of disability as something outside the norm. The narrative of "being pushed" becomes a footnote to the story of Roosevelt that has already been told via decades of mediated narration as a statesman and political figure. Narrating his disability does not upend the existing narrative. His political acumen is presented as disembodied, away from his body, because that is how Roosevelt was most often portrayed. The existing power structure is again maintained. Roosevelt's "legend" is secure.

Yet again, the de Certeauean cycle of faith to action is prominent. Roosevelt is "being pushed" so the audience can have faith in what they are seeing, but they need not take any action of/for Roosevelt as a disabled person, especially because he is deceased, but also because the disability has not been narrated to affect his power; the audience can "believe" (faith) and "do" (action) as though it has a negligible impact, if any at all. In other words, the absence of mediated narration about Roosevelt's disability strongly suggests the audience need not worry either. Neither journalist nor audience need to take bona fide action.

Mediated narration in this case does not provide the audience with any options toward change. It is likely the case that no options toward change are provided because to provide any would be to challenge the legacy that Roosevelt built for himself and the legacy that journalists mediated of/for Roosevelt during his lifetime and after his death. While it could be argued that showing Roosevelt in a wheelchair at all is in and of itself a form of social action by journalists, the audience is provided with little if any contextual background for what to do with this new information. Accordingly, the promise of critical theory to bring about meaningful social change is, at the very least, underutilized in this case.

**6. Sonny Weaver Sr.'s Body in *Draft Day* (2014)** The fictional movie *Draft Day* features a scene in which Sonny Weaver Sr., former coach of the National Football League's (NFL) Cleveland Browns, wishes to have his ashes scattered on the 50-yard line of a practice field named in his honor. Reflecting on his father's life, Kevin Costner's character, Sonny Weaver Jr., states: "Whoever thought it meant that much to him? Naming a simple practice field in his honor. God, he took pride in the weirdest things" (*Draft Day* 2014, 00:00:42–00:00:53).

Sonny Weaver Sr.'s body is evidence of an ongoing legacy: the timeless passage between father and son. The mentoring sports hero, in this instance Weaver Sr., is an unseen body celebrated for its potential. Most notable in Costner's narration of his father's body are the words "simple practice field" because those words point to what may be learned on that field, ostensibly through the course of hard work, and then applied during in-game situations. The work on the practice field, moreover, is usually out of view of the media world, which suggests an aversion to praise of the individual. Instead, in this example, as in Larkin's example above, the practice field will help the team (emphasis mine) to succeed as a unit. Recognizing his father's final wishes, Sonny Weaver Jr. comes to know his father as "proud" of the group above all else and, especially, proud of that group's potential—still unrealized but certainly realizable through work on the practice field. The narration provides the audience with only one option: remember Weaver Sr.'s legacy. Remembrance will not necessarily result in winning, though it certainly could. The legacy may be inspiring (similar to prayer) but it is difficult to measure whether the legacy will have any discernible impact on performance.

7. The *Cincinnati Enquirer*'s "Seven Days of Heroin" Reportage (2017)
On September 10, 2017, the *Cincinnati Enquirer* published "Seven Days of Heroin" on their website, detailing their weeklong reporting about the heroin epidemic in Ohio and northern Kentucky. As cultural theorist Michel de Certeau has articulated, "our society has become a recited society, in three senses: it is defined by stories . . . by citations of stories, and by the interminable recitation of stories" (1988, 186). Journalism as a social practice constructs a beginning, middle and end for the trials and tribulations of the human experience. The call to action in the *Enquirer* is to reflect and reinforce the fragile nature of life, especially when marred by drug use. As a case within new media technology history, the *Enquirer*'s reportage allows the members of the drug-afflicted community/ies to be the dialogic focus of the storytelling, often using individuals' own words to showcase the depth and breadth of the social problem. Storying "Seven Days of Heroin" in this manner emphasizes the importance of allowing affected individuals to narrate much of, or at least more of, their own stories, in order to help the audience make sense of the enormity of the problem. Such reportage allows for a consideration of the multiplicity of impact(s) that individuals struggling with drug use can have among and within their communities.

On April 16, 2018, the Pulitzer Prize for local reporting was awarded to the *Enquirer* for "Seven Days of Heroin." De Certeau has described the immersive quality of media narration: "Captured by the radio (the voice is the law) as soon as he awakens, the listener walks all day long through the forest of narrativities from journalism, advertising, and television, narrativities that still find time, as he is getting ready for bed, to slip a few final messages under the portals of sleep" (1988, 186). Journalism as a social practice is perhaps most notable for its omnipresent character: mediated narration is always available to help the audience make sense of the world and their place within it. The call to action in presenting the *Enquirer* staff with this award seems to be to underscore the importance of a different future for the drug-ravaged areas of Ohio and northern Kentucky. The presentation of this award to this story seems to emphasize the importance of a critical poststructuralist future for journalism, which allows a more diverse, pluralistic form of storytelling. Storying the Pulitzer win in this manner emphasizes the public service element of journalism as a mechanism through which audiences can more fully recognize challenges faced by individuals during times of crisis. This accolade elevates "Seven Days of Heroin" as an exemplar for journalism into the next decade and beyond.

"Seven Days of Heroin" especially captures the community impact of heroin use. The *Enquirer* introduces it in the following way:

> The Enquirer sent more than 60 reporters, photographers and videographers into their communities to chronicle an ordinary week in this extraordinary time.

Consider the following excerpt from the reportage:

> Lizzie Hamblin hasn't heard from her son, Scotty, since he walked out the night before. She's certain he's using heroin again. "Scott Hamblin Jr. I need to hear from you," Lizzie posts on her Facebook page. She calls him, too. And texts. Each message is more desperate than the last. "Call me." "I need you." "I need to hear you are alright." (*Cincinnati Enquirer*, sec. 11am, par. 5–9)

In this excerpt we are introduced to an ostensibly desperate mother; her dialogic process (dialogic attempts) of contact—through social media, telephone, text message—is revealed through the reportage, and we as the audience hear in her specific emotions the broader emotion of a community struggling with/through a public health crisis. The storytelling reveals the intertwined nature of the personal and the cultural: how they layer back onto one another to produce a fuller portrait of a deeper problem. In Hamblin's mother's struggle, we as the audience can understand the stress on the family. Mrs. Hamblin's story becomes one that we as an audience might imagine ourselves in, how difficult the waiting and uncertainty might feel to us were we in a similar situation.

Moreover, this reportage zeroes in on the history of a specific American problem during a particular American moment, providing historical context to a problem—heroin use—that might otherwise be too abstract and overwhelming for an audience to comprehend. The *Enquirer*'s reportage distills the problem down to its essence: the heroin epidemic has affected the relationship between Lizzie and her son Scotty. To understand the personal impact is to recognize the community impact. As the *Enquirer* reports, using a black and white box graphic, during the week of coverage there were "18 deaths, at least 180 overdoses, more than 200 heroin users in jail, 15 babies born with medical problems" (*Cincinnati Enquirer* 2017, 1).

Documentation of this community impact emphasizes that heroin is not a "one off" problem, something that can be avoided easily or something that is simply the result of poor choices of bad luck, but that it spreads across communities, communities like *ours*. We as the audience are drawn into the story: the *Enquirer*'s aspirational narrative seeks to shed light on a public health crisis in an American community in order to emphasize how this is an American problem that will demand an American solution. Before a solution can be devised, though, the community impact of the problem must be exposed. Journalism peels back the first layer in that process.

In providing such community exposure through this reportage, the dialogic ties that bind the community together (and the heroin epidemic that fractures the community) are revealed to the audience. In this way the reportage reveals that positive and negative forces are often in dialogic tension with one another (the people that want to save a community and the problems that want to tear it apart). This reportage provides a nuanced, complicated portrait of those enduring, deep-rooted challenges in a way that showcases the awareness-building, communitarian, and dialogic potential of longform narrative journalism. In de Certeauean terms, what is to be "believed" about Scotty Hamblin's body is that it has likely been harmed by heroin use. What is to be "done" is to work toward fixing the heroin problem by raising awareness about it through journalism like that completed by the *Enquirer*. In this seventh and final case, the de Certeauean journey from faith to action has brought about bona fide action that might eventually improve the lives of those affected by this crisis. In this case the promise of critical theory to bring about meaningful social change has been realized.

Each of the seven cases studied above reveals a power dynamic entrenched within its de Certeauean narrated reality. Most often the power dynamic explains the status quo in a way that reinforces its dominance. Indeed, the first six cases justify the existing structure and largely avoid discussing any deviation from the norm, or dismiss any such deviation as an aberration. Only the seventh case questions the power structure and works to begin unraveling it. Taken together these cases emphasize the need for a critical poststructuralist turn in journalism, in order to give voice to more diverse and pluralistic perspectives when storying the media world.

Video-sharing websites represent a trend among online media as "a hundred hours of video are uploaded to YouTube every minute" (Hermida 2016, 3). Accordingly, it is not surprising that some of the videos analyzed in this chapter were uploaded by news organizations to YouTube (www.youtube.com). Placing news content where individuals are ostensibly already spending their time is a logical strategy to gain their attention. The videos analyzed in this chapter demonstrate the "added value" of internet media (see, for example, Eighmey and McCord [1998]).

Three of the above cases demonstrate this principle especially well: (1) The two-minute-and-thirty-seven-second video time line of the Sandy Hook shootings provides visualizable context about how, where, and when the shootings occurred; (2) the twenty-three-second video of FDR "being pushed" visualizes his disability for an audience who may have rarely, if ever, seen Roosevelt's disabled body; and (3) the twenty-five-second video of the 911 call segment in "Seven Days of Heroin" helps the viewer visualize the specific place, this library, where one of the suspected drug overdoses took place. Each news story is effectively situated within a crisp, evocative imagistic package.

These three examples span five years (2012, 2013, 2017). They reflect the increasingly standardized usage of online videos to further explain specific elements of complex news stories. Each video complements the overarching story (the Sandy Hook shooting; FDR's presidency; the heroin epidemic), bringing meaning to particular elements of the story that can be rendered well in visual terms. (1) A video time line can ostensibly be produced to make meaning on a tight deadline; (2) archival footage of the president in a wheelchair represents his disabled status; and (3) images of a library help ground the disembodied voice of a 911 caller and allow the audience to make contextual sense of the library within the narrative.

Indeed, with the aid of video the online user has concrete moving pictures to visualize each of the stories in the above cases. New media technology history recognizes that while every medium was once new, its relative newness within a specific spatial-temporal context gave rise to particular consequences (see, for example, Silverstone [1999]). To make sense of that history is to unearth the affordances and constraints within which that history existed. The chapter uses the collective case study methodology (Stake 1994, 237) to investigate continuity and change across a seventeen-year period (1991–2018). Ultimately the chapter elevates instructive lessons from each of the case studies, about how and why power is made visible, or kept invisible, when storying the media world.

## De Certeau's Eligibility as Key to Representation

De Certeau's narrated reality strongly suggests that the concept of eligibility is the first criterion for representation. If a body is not deemed eligible by a decisionmaker or another arbiter of mediation, then it can arguably not even enter the arena of possibility within the realm of mediated narration. Eligibility is the dance card that is required to take the floor and begin moving, as it were, within this broader discourse. This criterion is significant because a broader array of considerations (space, time, place, limitations, boundaries, opportunities) would allow for a robust dialogue about athletic and corporeal success. When athletes have worn casts on their arms or masks on their faces, the act of doing so has occasionally provided them with a particular advantage in the course of a contest. It is worth imagining how disabled bodies may gain additive elements through technology/ies in a mainstream sports context. The technologized body may well make available an athletic edge that provides a performative advantage throughout the act of gameplay. The technologized body has potential to be exceptional.

When we use media, we furthermore do so with specific aims in mind (see, for example, Blumler and Katz [1974]). When disabled bodies go largely un(der)mediated, as they often did from 1991 through 2018, there is a sorely missed opportunity to broaden the media conversation about the varieties and realities of the athletic or nonathletic body. As communication scholar Norman K. Denzin has written, "Those who control the media control a society's discourses about itself" (1996, 319). Stating that represented bodies are not thorough is a minor act of resistance. It is also a minor declaration that mediated reality is not everyday reality.

Leaning especially on Denzin's cultural criticism, I assert that sports teaches us something about what is valued in society. When we only see the strong (usually male, usually white, usually able-bodied) athlete, it becomes too easy to disregard the intrinsic value of other bodies, especially disabled bodies. Recognizing my own autoethnographic position, I further worry about the broader sense of cultural leveling that may occur if we proceed down a path within which non-Mantlesque bodies are mostly absent from mediated narration. Especially in a cultural moment when American political elites are quick to decry certain coverage as "fake news," I worry about the implications of only presenting certain acceptable—however that term might be defined—bodies in mediated contexts. I thus call for a Christiansian pluralistic and multivocal consideration of the mediated body as a potential antidote to unnecessary leveling of the mediated body, and the need to avoid the characterization of only Mantlesque bodies as worthy of mediated narration.

Bringing James Carey into conversation with Denzin, critical media research has perhaps its strongest potential because, as Carey writes in *Communication as Culture*, "cultural studies make up a vehicle that can alter our self-image" (2009, 94). For any such Careyan alteration to occur, however, there must first be a close engagement with existing ways of knowing the cultural world in general and especially in mediated representations of the body. One of my aims in this chapter is to make meaningful strides in that direction. The Careyan call for self-image alteration is also a call to better bridge those two realities: the first which recognizes self-image as it exists (real) and the second which recognizes self-image as the media idealizes it (ideal). I humbly engage those who have reconsidered reason and its mediated variations, including perhaps most famously Neil Postman in the popular imagination, encouraging the incorporation of the body alongside the mind. My body, for example, could never have stood for as long as Lincoln and Douglas did in their debates.

There is a need for mediated consideration of the body, its potentials and limitations. Othered bodies fall out of line because they are not able to hold their place without taking a seat. Having actually physically fallen out of lines before—I am good at catching myself with my hands before I fall all the way down—I can confirm this has a physical impact—*it hurts*. Out of a minor act of resistance comes a minor declaration which allows me to speak to the following minor truth: to make space for othered bodies is to recognize and embrace the pluralistic, multivocal, authentic, and ultimately Christiansian conceptualization of the body. For Christians the body is arguably inextricably linked to both mind and spirit in order to capture its full sense of agency and potential. The body is always on a journey, not necessarily always forward as it may be falling, but always in a sense of flux and fluidity. Moving and carrying to the next position. Progressing toward a more intentional way of knowing the body within the human experience.

Critical theory has a vital role to play in this process of fuller representation. As critical theorist Mark Poster has written: "Unlike some poststructuralist tendencies, critical theory springs from an assumption that we live amid a world of pain, that much can be done to alleviate that pain, and that theory has a crucial role to play in that process" (1989, 3). Affirming more bodies, including disabled bodies, as eligible for participation in a de Certeauean–narrated reality would make significant strides toward alleviating the pain of exclusion from the representational landscape. Just as I noted earlier in the chapter, I struggled against my body to take a picture in Minneapolis, and I know that my body (or yours) might face further struggles ahead as well. I share this book with you, dear reader, in the modest hope of a representational future for a host of bodies—heroic and abled like Mantle's, fragile and disabled like FDR's or my own—and all sorts of bodies in between. If Camus was right, and I suspect he was, about the fleeting, fragile nature of any sort of corporeal or geographic paradise (mine, yours, ours) then it seems to me that a Christiansian approach to authentic disclosure is even more important. I offer this book, reaching toward the promise that future journalists and journalism(s) might more holistically encapsulate what it means to be a mediated being in a mediated body. In doing so, our bodies have potential to help us each more readily carry the essence of the human experience. The stories in this chapter and in this book are stories not dissimilar to mine in some ways.

Denzin is right when he articulates that we always bring ourselves to our research, whether we admit doing so or not. As he writes in *Interpretive Interactionism*: "The researcher is historically and locally situated within the very processes being studied" (1989, 3). There are both celebrated and unrecognized heroes examined in the media coverage considered in this book. Their coverage presents only a cracked-open window into the entirety of their impact. The broader project of this work is a call for fuller representation of those individuals we think we know, and initial representation of those individuals whom we have yet to learn about among the media audience. I am delighted to invite you along on this journey toward more robust, multivocal representation in mediated narration. Engaging in this massive undertaking is definitely a challenging task, but the potentials of and for the human experience to shine more robustly through the tapestry of cultural storytelling is well worth the effort.

## Conclusion

The findings of the cases in this chapter reveal my overall thesis: (1) mediated narration most often uncritically elevates the characteristics that have made the individuals or institutions powerful as justification for why they "must be believed"; (2) mediated narration tends to prescribe actions for audience members that either do not disturb the existing power structure or serve to reinforce the existing power structure ("what must be done"); and (3) the implications of the prescribed actions most often have little, if any, potential to promote meaningful social change. The critical exception to this rule is the case of the "Seven Days of Heroin" reportage by the staff of the *Cincinnati Enquirer*, which received the 2018 Pulitzer Prize for local reporting. I assert that this case indicates the need for a critical, poststructuralist turn in journalism, to foreground histories, biographies, and lived experiences. Indeed, "Seven Days of Heroin" strongly suggests that digital media production and consumption have untapped potential. Taking this case as exemplar, the process of storying the media world can more holistically represent the ways individuals and institutions engage with one another during times of crisis and throughout everyday life.

# 2 Storying Sandy Hook

I embrace my position in the world (see Alcoff [1988]), and my myriad identities (see Rambo [2005]) include the following: a researcher, a teacher, a servant to the academy and my community, a brother, a son, an uncle, a partner, a white heterosexual male, a disabled person, a sports fan, among many other intersecting and overlapping identities. Most notable for the purposes of this study are my identities as a researcher, a disabled person, and a sports fan. Like philosopher Susan Wendell, I "experience the world as structured for people who have no weaknesses" (1989, 104). My weaknesses sometimes force me to make other plans. Cultural theorist Michel de Certeau writes: "The weak must continually turn to their own ends forces alien to them" (1988, xix). Inspired by de Certeau, I view this process as a certain kind of pleasure: the art of more fully making space for one's self in the world.

I was eight years old on October 27, 1991. That evening the Minnesota Twins won the World Series. Gene Larkin, a pinch hitter, stepped to the plate in the bottom of the tenth inning and delivered a base hit into left field. Larkin was a person whose story was actually unfolding on the screen alongside mine. The only thing I remember about that night is that I felt tired. I was watching the game on television. I was probably very excited when Larkin got his hit—I was a big fan—but I don't remember excitement. I do not remember screaming, shouting or making any exclamations whatsoever in that moment. If I stayed awake the whole game, and I believe I did, wakefulness alone in that state seems like victory itself. In truth, ten innings is a long time for an eight-year-old to stay awake. Today, I just watched Larkin's hit again on YouTube. I didn't feel any sense of excitement when Larkin stepped to the plate, or when he lifted the ball into left field. I know how the story ends. Mediated recollection allows me to place this particular memory into a broader narrative. I reach for my bookshelf, find Em Griffin's *A First Look at Communication*

*Theory*, which I use when I teach Communication Theory. Turning first to Walter Fisher, I eventually settle on Marshall McLuhan. Interpreting McLuhan, Griffin writes, "Media not only extend our reach and increase our efficiency, they also act as a filter to organize and interpret our social existence" (2003, 344). Watching YouTube, I am able to place the details of Larkin's hit into fuller focus. It was the bottom of the tenth, the base hit traveled to left field. My excitement today is not in the event, but in the opportunity to sharpen it, to recall precisely how the story ends.

This October will mark twenty-nine years since Larkin's hit, since the Twins' last World Series. The communication technologies which allow me to watch the hit were not in use then, but I can look today and see the seeds of an interest in media and in the audience. Invoking philosopher Sophia Isako Wong, I recognize that "this is a deeply personal piece of philosophy, not a sociological survey; others have spoken and will speak for themselves elsewhere" (2002, 92). Wong is writing about her brother, who has Down Syndrome. I am writing this chapter; I have cerebral palsy. Watching Larkin in '91, I wasn't tired because of my disability; I was tired because it was late. Watching YouTube, I recognize how important that '91 Twins team was to me. If they won in seven games, and they did, then I could do anything. Their victory opened a path forward for me through persistence. Returning to Griffin's interpretation of McLuhan, I am more persuaded today than I have ever been by the conviction that "nothing remains untouched by communication technology" (2003, 344). Following Susan Wendell, "I have a particular standpoint determined in part by both my physical condition and my social situation" (1989, 106). I use personal memory to recreate the experience of being an eight-year-old watching game seven in Rochester, about two hours south of the stadium. I use YouTube to confirm, but also to build a dialogue between my childhood and adult selves, in recognition of my standpoint. Telling these two stories—Larkin in 1991 and YouTube in 2016—I realize that I am "no longer in the story" (Brison 2008, 197) of my youth. What I have gained, though, is a fuller appreciation for it.

As Sarah Symonds LeBlanc has perceptively observed, "By sharing narratives, social constructivists explore and make sense of the world around them" (2016, 111). By examining these cases, studying the narratives therein and exploring their findings and significance, I take up that project in this chapter and this book. Inspired by Adrienne Rich, I assert we are "living in the earth deposits of our history" (3). This chapter is especially motivated by the power of story. Following Carolyn Ellis , I "realize that every story is partial and situated" (1999, 673). Moreover, I recognize the central position of the media in the chapter and in this book. Accordingly, I am also investigating McLuhan's assertion that "it is the medium that shapes and controls the scale and form of human interaction and association" (1994, 9). To this point, as one example that is especially tied to poetry, autoethnography and media, consider the following case: In W. S. Merwin's "James," I especially admire the first two lines of the five-line poem: "News comes that a friend far away / is dying now" (2005, 255). These lines seem especially fitting for the way they reveal blurring boundaries between media and memory. Media are evoked through Merwin's use of the word *news*.

Within the definition of news, I count news about death as among the most pressing information. While a core element of the human experience, death (especially when it occurs in unexpected circumstances) is nonetheless jarring, particularly for the way that it can evoke feelings of deep loss and recognition of one's own inevitable mortality. Merwin's two lines evoke memory not only because of the form of his writing itself, but also because of the compact nature of the expression.

As storytellers in the media world, we tell stories through their form as much as their content. I am thinking about Shannon and Weaver's Sender-Message-Channel-Receiver Model (7). I am thinking about the channels (platforms) through which we produce and consume media content. In the ways we produce and consume media content, we live with and through the media world. In other words, we are living with and through our chosen channels. This way of knowing makes autoethnography an effective methodological lens in studying the media. The first time I went rock climbing was in elementary or middle school. I went to the same school for prekindergarten through seventh grade, so the years all blend together. I remember climbing, and making it to the top, and being surprised at my own strength.

If I have the dates correct in my mind, I went rock climbing for the first time between the ages of ten and fourteen, just a few years after I was profiled as "not your average 9-year-old" ("Faces in the Crowd" 1993, par. 1) in the local newspaper. The article began: "Peter Gloviczki puts his heart and mind into everything he does, even playing with classmates on the grounds of Lincoln at Mann School. The 9-year-old, born prematurely and with cerebral palsy, inspires others with his love of life" (par. 1). I felt then (and continue to feel) that the article captured my optimism. As a journalism and mass communication researcher and teacher, I now also recognize the fact that my news story aligned with a "human interest" style of "soft" news (Gans 2004, 28). I hope that the news story about me helped children (and adults) reimagine limitations and possibilities.

Barbara Jago opens her autoethnography "The Car Radio: An Autoethnographic Short Story" with the following question: "How much longer 'til we get there?" (2004, 1). As I author this book, that question is alive in my mind as well. I console myself with a simple truth: journeying is an always incomplete process—its allure alive in the fact that it is never fully finished.

I owe my autoethnographic turn to Dr. John Youngblood, who asked me, on a snowy February day in Potsdam, New York, if I had ever considered writing about my body in an autoethnographic manner. Not only was I relatively unfamiliar with autoethnography at the time (almost ten years ago) but, speaking truthfully, I also hated the question. To that point, I had wrongly considered the process of writing about myself as unnecessarily reductive; I worried that focusing on the singular self would reduce the overall impact of my writing to myself. What I have recognized since then—and most fully through the process of writing this book—is that incorporating the self from a research perspective is a source of strength. In other words, revealing the self is a liberating practice within interpretive, reflexive autoethnographic inquiry.

Kathy Tanabe helped me walk independently. For several years she came to my elementary school to provide me physical therapy. In my mind's eye I can still see walking with her to/from room to room of the school. When I went back to visit I was shocked at how small the school seemed. The vantage point of youth and innocence makes everything seem larger than it actually is/was, or at least this was my lived experience of my elementary school. I took my first freestanding steps around age five: walking across my parents' master bedroom, before I fell into my mother's waiting arms. I am guesstimating these details. I remember most vividly that there was a jet-black bedframe in my parents' master bedroom. I have a memory of my mother sitting on the edge of the bed with arms outstretched waiting to catch me, but I do not actually possess documentation in the form of a photograph of this memory or the event taking place. The recollection is the essential truth of how I remember the event today, thirty or so years after it happened. Interpretation leads me to regard this event as a seminal moment in my lifeworld, because it afforded me the pragmatic ability to be my own engine of movement for ostensibly the first time in my life. Placing that experience into its proper context is one of this book's "epiphanies" (Ellis, Adams, and Bochner 2011, par. 9).

Though I don't recall if it was Kathy who released me into my mother's outstretched embrace or not, she is the first physical therapist in my young imagination. I have been thinking, as I reflect on this vignette, about the strength of interpretation as a methodological tool within a qualitative researcher's toolkit (see, for example, Denzin and Lincoln [1994]). The memories are sharp in my recollection and yet the most I can do is remember that I am recalling them correctly (Wall 2008, 45). Other physical therapists helped me gain a sense of very early balance, using their hands, arms, wrists, and wooden sticks—more like large poles—among other kinds of apparatus. Reflecting on this experience today, I am compiling in my mind the notion that working through physical disability, especially during youth, is a sort of do-it-yourself aesthetic of guess and check work. I both admire this reality and am baffled by it: I wish there was a more streamlined way to aid those families with disabilities, to help them make decisions that were better informed by past precedent(s). In this context, I hope to write into the space between theory and practice in order to provide actionable ideas for a multivocal presentation of athletic and disabled bodies across mediated narration. I am working to be relevant to students and scholars and to engage allied members of the general public as well.

I remember striding across my parents' master bedroom and falling into my mother's arms. I do not think I realized until my twenties what a meaningful achievement this represented in my life and in my medical and family care. In terms of a milestone, this event made mobility considerably more attainable for me. Most disabled people I've known have stories similar to mine. My friend Whitney, for example, is a wheelchair user with cerebral palsy, a person who continually inspires me with her pursuit of physically rigorous activities like boxing and surfing, among other activities. We write in admiration of those who helped us gain acceptance (our own and others'). The list of individuals who have inspired me in this way is far too numerous to mention. I have experienced great generosity and a sense of profound giving at every level of my schooling and work life. Our stories have also intertwined self and social, with varying degrees of recognition (see, for example, Reed-Danahay [2017]).

Sutures give me time on my own two feet. After hamstring-lengthening surgery, the gift of walking more easily unaided, without a hand as much or as often. My early teens. Des'ree's "You Gotta Be" is one of my many anthems, and I use the song to push on. Reading this memory against the backdrop of the FDR footage, I recognize that music is one way I push myself (the active pushing instead of the passive being pushed). As a boy with cerebral palsy, I want to inspire without being inspirational. Growing up in the Midwest, I don't know any place with public transit. There is, more recently, a push for public transit in Minneapolis–St. Paul, but that's not something that was in my imagination as a child. I didn't know to want that at the time.

Lennard J. Davis persuasively writes in *The Disability Studies Reader*, "The idea of a norm is less a condition of human nature than it is a feature of a certain kind of society" (2016, 2). The body is valued according to the spaces that it can (or cannot) inhabit. To make space for a body, to make it able to be visible, is to assign it at least a modicum of value. Bodies stifled by erasure or invisibility cannot fully articulate themselves or their potentialities. Narratives must be allowed and encouraged to transgress across and outside of the lines, because the lines were inevitably drawn before them, and without them in mind.

Otherly-abled bodies represent the unexpected but nonetheless usually welcome guests. As David J. Bodenhamer writes, "Humans organize space by using the body as a reference point, and our language contains numerous words—up, down, left, right, back, forward, etc.—that keep us physically oriented to the environment we are in" (2015, 13). In other words, I recognize (and worry) that a body that does not have full movement might not always be recognized or valued as a full body. Mediated representations are meaningful, as a result, for the way that they might trouble, limit or expand existing sociocultural conceptions of a body and its boundaries and/or potentials. For conceptual growth to occur, the boundaries must always be malleable. Disabled people and their loved ones know this fact quite well, as do educational practitioners who value ongoing development. To engage toward any reality like barrier-free access, the reality that there will always be some barriers must be recognized. The core issue then becomes which barriers can be overcome, and how might we as a sociocultural unit place those barriers into order from smallest to largest, tackling the "low-hanging fruit" first in order to build momentum. Such activities represent generational work, but the work of living ultimately and thankfully spans the boundaries of a single earthly life, as well as the usually understood domestic, geographic boundaries of work/home or here/away, respectively.

At its baseline, the mission of this study is to make the vulnerable more visible and do so with respect in the spirit of communitarian dialogue. I begin with visibility because it is a manageable, pragmatic, accomplishable task. Media have opened cultural conversations about the Other for some time now, and visibility possesses within it the core ability to make the strange more familiar. Most specifically, to make visible is to unstrange what was once unknown into a series of knowable components, which the viewer's eye can then use to identify parts as one builds the whole. A body adorned with surgical scars, as mine is and yours may also be, is recognizable once those scars are located and their impact is mapped. And the language that one uses to employ when revealing those scars (adorned versus littered with) also positions the audience for a certain sort of reading about that corporeal reality.

Narratives and their narrators teach audiences how to read their significance. While learning requires close engagement and a healthy sense of diligence, this dialogic bond is not only possible but ultimately worthwhile. In this way, it is worth underscoring the notion that bodies are almost always authored at least to some extent by those individuals who inhabit them. Narratives may be coauthored by the cultural contexts in which they are immersed (I can walk freely on blacktop but not on ice) but I have at least a voice in how my body is narrated based on how/if I position it to/for the camera in particular or media in general. Once I have completed that positioning, I must however surrender the outcome of the positioning to the audience who will inevitably and sometimes unfortunately respond to it as they will.

I make corporeal choices in the service of caring for broader lived experiences. My mind is always tethered to muscle and bones. Amber Lauren Johnson has written instructively about reconciliation in a corporeal context: "Be a body on the line. But I know how bodies on the line are treated" (2017, 94). Considering this advice in a slightly different context than did Johnson, I draw my body frail and flimsy as it sometimes is, in its most often context: seated. I sit out of necessity. To be a body on the line might for me mean to be standing, active, taking action. Though I am a positive, uplifting, uplifted academic, I occasionally feel guilt that I am not more clearly on the line: I should be standing for those who cannot stand, I think to myself, when my love the lovely Jenny asks if I want to go to a protest. Or more specifically, she says something along the lines of how she is thinking of going. She does not ask me directly. I read her not asking as an act of mercy. She knows the act of asking would make my muscles and my soul sweat. She wants to stand for poor people's rights in Columbia, the capital of our adopted home state. I want her to do that, too. I wish I could stand for that, for anything, in protest. I have to reconcile in a Johnsonian context that standing for long periods of time is physically draining for me. But you can physically stand, Peter, I think to myself, when others cannot.

This internal dialogue is chock-full of a sense of doubt about whether and to what extent I am doing enough with the body I am lucky enough to possess. Structures of resistance demand a great deal from bodies but are not orchestrated with them in mind. When I was at the London School of Economics I had to cut lines all the time. I did not have a choice: my soul wanted to queue up where my body could not. My body often if not always takes the lead in similar situations. And yet I recognize that, like M. Francyne Huckaby, I am always aided by the technology around me. There is truth in Huckaby's words: "My senses assimilate to the technology that records and re-creates light, moving images and sound" (2017, 340). I humbly am raised up because of the people, structures, relationships, technologies, platforms, and devices that bolster me. These modes of assistance compensate where spaces may fail me (Bodenhamer, Corrigan, and Harris 2015). In this way, I am muscle, bones, and technologies, blended in some configuration. All these entities, living and mechanistic, form the community that carries me, that walks alongside me in the world. I write to and for and with them: to remember and commemorate and acknowledge my affinity for them (Richardson 2007). The corporeal expands, as it must, beyond itself: being technologized, the self is today also always social. The act of reconciling such braiding is the order of the day and a deeply vital task, as we near the second decade of our second millennium. Reconciliation, making meaning of the past, is also a building block to be completed in the service of imagining and then enacting the upcoming, ongoing opportunities. In the service of imagining a future.

I feel an intense sadness over the fact that after the Columbine High School shooting in Littleton, Colorado, more than twenty years ago, school shootings became part of American culture. The victims of school shootings have lost the opportunity to imagine a future for themselves. I write this autoethnographic vignette as a way to cope with that sense of sadness, which I believe might be shared by educators around the country and the world. To be a teacher today is to live in the truth that during the course of a lesson, a person might burst through the classroom door with high-powered weapons and inflict carnage on the students and teachers inside. I study school shootings in an attempt to make sense of it all, realizing that my years of training are more likely to reveal perplexing questions than solid answers. And still, I write. In hopes that I might bring into being a more just and free and secure teaching environment. All the while holding my nose at the fact that justice and freedom and security need to be uttered in a pedagogical context in 2021.

I've never myself participated in lockdown drills in schools. At thirty-six I'm old enough to have mercifully missed their institutionalization into the academy. I do believe such drills are valuable; I am simply trying to honor my own vulnerability and fallibility in making that admission. I offer this chapter in hopes that it might contribute to a fuller understanding of coverage of school shootings in the media world.

As autoethnographer Cris Davis has written: "Stories are a way of knowing and communicating; we connect with each other through our stories" (2008, 415). Though I study digital memorialization and sense-making Sandy Hook made me angry in a deeper way than earlier violence. The targets of the shooting, elementary school children, seemed especially defenseless to me. Any murder is senseless, of course, but Sandy Hook activated something deeper within me. Writing this chapter, I thought of Davis's words and of my own vulnerability as a young disabled boy at my elementary school. I attended the same school for nine years (from prekindergarten through seventh grade) and I was transported via memory back to my pre-K class, where I remember an afternoon assignment involving cutting a piece of paper. Manual tasks are still challenging for me today, and were especially so in my youth.

It was around 2:30 or so in the afternoon on the day in my memory, a time that matters because it rests in the psychic moment when even a young boy knows dismissal is near. It was almost time to go home. I was holding scissors as the fire alarm went off. I remember the paraprofessional (a classroom aide) assigned to work with me grabbed the scissors and more or less carried me out of the room. There was no fire, it was just a drill—a stupid drill, I feel like we had them once a week growing up—a reminder that the body is a lot of moving parts. The paraprofessional helped me get where I was going, got me outside. I am terrified for the Sandy Hook children, for anyone who might need a hand during a drill or God forbid in the moment itself. The lack of mobility affordances reveals an abject sense of need; humans or machines are needed to stand in for the elements that one's body (or mine) cannot do on its own. The body becomes its own constraint, unable to act as its own agent of change, corporeal connections to other kinds of sociocultural apparatus. I feel connected to them within the memory of my own relatively benign pre-K experience. Remembering the vulnerable boy I was thirty years ago binds me to them, makes me grieve for them. Such vulnerability also encourages me to try and chart an intentional, actionable path toward fuller reportage.

### Sensemaking and Narrative Media

My purpose here is to present an operational fictions analysis of the case of the 2012 CBS News Sandy Hook Timeline Coverage. Stuart Hall's concept of operational fiction is the most appropriate theoretical lens for this analysis because it recognizes that mediated narration seeks to foreground a specific narrative about media power, which influences how audiences make sense of news coverage. Hall asserts: "Objectivity, like impartiality, is an operational fiction. All filming and editing is the manipulation of raw data—selectively perceived, interpreted, signified" (1974, 23). I further follow Hall in asserting that journalistic storytelling is an assemblage of meaning(s) strung together to tell a specific story. As Hall states, "each decision to link this piece of film with that, to create a discourse out of the disparate fragments of edited material, makes sense only within a logic of exposition" (23). Narrative storytelling provides the context to bridge one word to the next, one scene to the next; to bridge in this way is, quite precisely, to build a news story. As Hall states, "we decode its significance—it cannot literally be 'read off' the denoted images themselves—in terms of these contexts of awareness, in terms of the connotative power of the message" (24). Hall is seeking to consider the power-brokering element of narrativization and his insights provide an instructive lens for analysis. This theory is instructive for this analysis in three ways: (1) it helps identify operational fictions in the news narration; (2) it helps decode the significance of the operational fictions; and (3) it recognizes that those operational fictions strongly support a sense-making of false completion.

Robert E. Stake's model of an intrinsic case study provides the methodological lens for this case: "In what we may call an intrinsic case study, study is undertaken because one wants a better understanding of this particular case" (1994, 237). Stake further specifies: "It is an integrated system. The parts do not have to be working well, the purposes may be irrational, but it is a system" (236). Here I study the case of CBS News's time line coverage of the Sandy Hook shooting for its intrinsic lessons about journalism and mass communication in times of crisis. I have, in fact, made a deliberate methodological choice to pair Stake's intrinsic case study methodology with Hallian analysis of operational fictions, introduced above. Just as Hall was writing in Britain during the early 1970s, a time of great violence in Northern Ireland, I am writing in America during the early 2020s, a time of too frequent school shootings. Put simply, Hall's theoretical lens appears culturally applicable to the American moment being studied here. I am also motivated by Hall's cross-cultural considerations of power as a social force that was given to and removed from those elements most heavily mediated in discourse communities. From my reading of Hall, it strikes me that power is a transactional currency that has the opportunity to either construct or deconstruct the elements that it acts upon within the context of operational fiction. To study the "system" of this specific case of reportage is to better understand why certain cases rise to social media prominence, as this one did.

Twenty-year-old Adam Lanza launched his massacre at home. Officials say Lanza shot his mother Nancy multiple times, killing her in her bed. Lanza then took four guns, legally registered to his mother, and drove this black Honda to Sandy Hook elementary school about five miles away. Students there had finished reciting the Pledge of Allegiance. And the building's doors had been locked. Then, around nine-thirty Friday morning, staffers in the front office heard popping noises. Police say those were likely the sounds of Lanza shooting out the glass of one of the school doors. Lanza entered the building, carrying a Bushmaster AR-15 assault rifle, with two semi-automatic handguns inside the pockets of his military style cargo pants. Police say he was also carrying hundreds of rounds of ammunition in multiple magazines. There were more popping sounds. Someone in the front office keyed the microphone on the school's public address system in a frantic attempt to sound a warning. As the gunfire continued, 911 calls were made. And just before 9:36, a police dispatcher radioed the first alert. 6–7 Sandy Hook School, caller is indicating she thinks there's someone shooting in the building. The precise sequence of what happened next is unclear. But we do know, Lanza headed down a hallway, towards the section of the school containing the classrooms of the youngest students. There, he killed twenty first graders. Shooting all of them numerous times, with the .223 assault rifle. Six adult women including the principal, the school psychologist, and teachers were also killed. Police radio logs suggest the shooting lasted about ten minutes. The slaughter ended as the first police officers arrived on the scene. Sources say Lanza was briefly spotted at the end of a hallway. He ducked from view. The officers heard a final volley of shots. Lanza had used one of the handguns to take his own life. ATF officials now tell us Lanza and his mother went shooting together at various ranges over the past several years. But Scott, they still don't know if Adam Lanza practiced in recent weeks. Bob, you mentioned that there was a fourth gun, do the investigators have any theory on what he intended to do with that? Well, that fourth gun, it was a shotgun capable of carrying a large drum of ammunition. Lanza, when he went into the school, left it behind in the car's trunk. Police say they're not sure what he intended to do with it, Scott, but it suggests maybe he was thinking about a broader attack. Bob, thanks very much. ("Newtown Massacre" 2012, 00:00:00–00:02:38)

## Five Operational Fictions

Analysis reveals five "operational fictions" (Hall 1974, 23) in this news reportage:

*Time-line-as-beginning is the first operational fiction.*

The details are told with specific attention to where they were "launched." Even though Lanza "launched" at home that day, the school shooting arguably began the moment that Lanza started planning it. Articulating the beginning of the school shooting as Orr does, on the day of the event itself, erases an entire history of events that led up to that day. Moreover, to tell the story as Orr does is to obscure at best, or ignore at worst, the often intersecting past(s)-present(s)-future(s) that are likely to underscore a major event like a school shooting.

*Shooting-as-"massacre" is the second operational fiction in this news reportage.*

To characterize the shooting (the act Lanza engaged in) as a massacre is to emphasize the "indiscriminate killing" that is at the heart of a definition of a massacre. The reporter, Orr, could have simply said: "Lanza killed his first victim, his mother, at home." But instead he chose the more stylized articulation "launched his massacre." Selecting the word *massacre* is a form of rhetorical violence—a phrase more suited to the Hollywood blockbuster film than to the murder of innocent children.

*"Officials say" as vague authority is the third operational fiction in this news reportage.*

The use of the term "officials say" gives the audience no choice but to accept the authority of the journalistic organization, and it also serves to reinforce the power of the journalistic organization, placing it at the center of the reportage rather than allowing the story its full due. Orr could have indicated the main authority (the name or title of the individual) who conveyed that information, but he did not do that. The use of this phrase "officials say" is vague and it binds the audience into an unreasonable amount of trust in this story.

*"Drove this black Honda" (or, when meaningless information masquerades as significant) is the fourth operational fiction in this news reportage.*
Orr mentions the black Honda and shows a picture of a black vehicle (ostensibly Lanza's) to show the audience how Lanza ostensibly traveled from his home to the school. The mode of transportation, while related to the story, is arguably trivial. Put simply, a car is a car. Prioritizing the make and model of an everyday vehicle in the first three sentences of the story is to suggest that the way Lanza got to the school is more important than what happened when he got there. Again, such prioritization is more closely suited to a Hollywood blockbuster than to the murder of innocent children. Such an apparently flippant decision—disguising meaningless information as significant—prioritizes the journalist over the subject.

*News-as-reassurance is the fifth operational fiction in this news reportage.*
The details are recounted in a steady tone, so as to emphasize what is already known to the public. The steady tone in journalist Bob Orr's voice is ostensibly an attempt to stabilize an otherwise unstable situation. News as reassuring performance comes through in the way that Orr voices this excerpt from the story. Reassurance is prominent through the process of sharing facts in chronological order. Orr shares information with the ease of a practiced journalist. The facts of the news story and the verbal clock that is its chronology ground the story in its familiar, recognizable narration. The viewer or listener may wander in and out of Orr's narrative before always finding their way safely back. Orr's narrative anchors the viewer or listener into a particular conceptualization of events.

## Decoded Significance in These Operational Fictions

In this reportage each of these five operational fictions has a decoded significance, a strongly suggested reading of their meaning.

Time-line-as-beginning seems to indicate that the journalists know how it all started, a fact about which they are most likely ignorant and about which no information is provided. Orr could have prefaced the story by saying, "We don't know how it all started, but this is what happened on the day of the shooting." There is no distinction between what is known and what is unknown. To express a "launch," as Orr does, is cognitively alluring but factually incorrect.

Shooting-as-"massacre" strongly suggests indiscriminate killing (a definition of that word). While some mass shooters in the past seventy-five years may have been killing indiscriminately (see on this topic, for example, DeFoster [2017]), Lanza appears to have been focused on killing at this particular school. Therefore, this term appears to be factually inaccurate. A more descriptive, rather than emotive, word, such as "targeted attack," seems better suited in this instance. Furthermore, there is no turn toward "biography" (Christians 2007, 126) (who was killed), which seems to take the attention away from the victims and onto the event of the "massacre." The implications of this word choice are that Lanza (who carried out the "massacre") appears more important than his victims.

"Officials say" arguably confuses an audience seeking to have their informational needs met, because it is a vague statement that affirms the power of the journalist and the media organization. In other words, the journalists have used the vague phrase to enact a reality that is semantically private. The journalists or their editors or producers likely know the source, but that information is not being shared with the audience. Put simply, there is no clear attempt at dialogue about who "said" the information. As a result there may be a decreased level of trust between journalist and audience.

"The Black Honda" is an example of a journalist claiming to provide important details without actually helping an audience more fully make sense of the event's significance. Orr recites the make and model of the car with conviction, but the reality constructed through this narration is hollow—the car is not an accessory to the crime, it is simply a mechanical vessel to carry a person from point A to point B. To include it in this story is to feign diligence in reportage. I further assert the detail about the car to be false "biography" because the make and model have no outcome on the murder of children.

"News-as-reassurance" reinforces the paternalistic distance between

Orr and the audience. The journalist with his steady voice will ostensibly "take care" of the audience by providing them with details about what happened. Orr could have begun the report by saying "stories like this are hard to report on," but he did not. Orr's lack of vocal emotive expression reinforces a detached narrator unfazed by the murder of children that has occurred.

Across all five of these "operational fictions," this Hallian operational fiction analysis builds understanding about the power of mediated narration in relation to the Sandy Hook shootings. These findings strongly suggest that mediated narration risks superficial reportage about meaningful dialogues (like the shootings) unless considerable words, chronology, and images are devoted to multivalent portrayals of complicated issues, such as school shootings in times of crisis. Longform narrative journalism about complicated issues, over multiple days and multiple locations, has the potential to achieve a fuller sense of the scope of the story, its victims, and its aftermath. In doing so, the complicated elements of challenging narratives might also be braided into specific elements of a broader tapestry.

### Mediated Narration as False Completion

Among the most significant journalistic practices is the leveling effect of placing a multitude of unrelated stories in quick succession to one another as part of a television news broadcast. I consider this style of news reading almost mundane, because it has become so ingrained into the American and Western culture of the television news genre as to be considered "common sense" (Hall 1974, 23). The overarching problem with this style is that news items become fairly well interchangeable, at constant risk of losing their specific content meanings and broader contextual significance(s). I am interested in what it might mean to reconstitute the present in a more pluralistic manner. As a critical media scholar, I worry that the voices at the forefront of mediated experience do little more than reinforce existing hierarchies of power and control. And importantly, though not surprisingly, this power dynamic is not only an historical artifact. As an example from a more recent moment, in a 2018 news story a British news outlet, the *Guardian*, wrote about the U.S. school shooting epidemic: "The repeated tragedies and frightening incidents continue to spark deeply divided political responses, with some Americans urging tighter laws on gun sales and ownership and others advocating for putting more armed guards in schools, or making it easier for teachers and parents to carry their own concealed weapons" (2018, 1).

This passage is factually accurate and in keeping with journalistic norms and the tradition of objectivity. But I wish to dig deeper, following Hall's lead. The passage suggests that there are two sides, "This or That" (Hall 1974, 23). This passage (and much of present-day American journalism) exhibits a gross overconfidence in its levels of certainty. There are these two sides in the gun debate, of course, but I might imagine other (equally valuable) perspectives as well. Complex issues require a multivalent perspective. Taking the critical poststructuralist perspective presented in this chapter, when mediated narration oversimplifies complexity, as in the *Guardian* passage and in the Sandy Hook example presented above, mediated narration erases an opportunity for meaningful debate on any or all sides of this issue. Put simply, the quest for certainty ("two sides") (Hall 1974, 22) yields a false sense of completion in the reportage. Allowing for manifold "sides," as many as are needed in a given situation, has stronger potential to be a fruitful approach on a case-by-case basis.

Failing to fully narrate about the victims, to mention them by name, cause their loss to blend somewhat into the background of the story. The victims are not directly addressed. The shooter (Lanza) and his mother are the humans in the foreground of this reportage. Accordingly, the story prioritizes the shooter over the victims. While I assume the prioritization may occur because of ready access to visuals, storying this tragedy without the victims compounds their deaths in an even more concrete manner. Their loss of life is amplified by another loss: the loss of their narrative stories upon their deaths. Structuring the storying of the Sandy Hook shootings in this way also repeats a fairly worn narrative about school shootings: that is, a story told from the perspective of the shooter. In doing so the narrative elevates the shooter over the victims. In other words, the narrative power in this storying process reinforces the shooter's position. Upon the amplification of the shooter's position, the narratives of any others (victims, bystanders, community members) recede into relative obscurity, so that audiences find it difficult to gain a firm grasp of what happened and how it happened. Organizing the reportage in this manner weakens the perceived value of the victims.

Visualizing school shootings carries little risk (the shooting has already taken place) and offers fairly high ratings. The human drama embedded in the story is inevitable, as the story represents the worst possible outcome any parent, or any student, could likely imagine. Although every school shooting is an unspeakable tragedy, Sandy Hook is all the more so because of the age of the children who were killed. Their stories were not adequately told in the case examined here, which leads to their being vaguely, rather than directly, mourned. Though this weakening may be unintentional, without the mention of the victims their bodies lose any discernible power, represented only through vague and quantified spoken reference. Numbers never die; people do. I mention the quantification of the victims here because expressing lives as numerals compares them, perhaps unintentionally, to entries on a spreadsheet. Their stories are told only through a collective number, stripped of any of the components—a name, a hometown, a photo, a birthday—we know as everyday elements for children within the human experience.

Recognizing that school-shooting reportage often follows this basic trope, I must ask as a critical/cultural scholar whether we have reached in school shooting reportage what my friend and colleague critical/cultural scholar Jasmine B. Ulmer has called in another context "legacies of injustice" (2017, 386). Though Ulmer was referring to the city of Detroit in the American state of Michigan, media audiences know how stories about school shootings tend to be portrayed, just as they know how the city of Detroit tends to be portrayed: through overutilized, reductive, and painfully simplified language. The opportunity that is missed—overlooked accidentally or on purpose—is, in the case of Sandy Hook, the rich storying of the lives that were lost. Save for the number, in fact, which is little more than an oblique gesture that there were lives lost, there is precious little storying of these dead children at all. The Ulmerian "legacy of injustice" in this situation, therefore, is that these children are not portrayed as innocent and vulnerable, but are not sufficiently portrayed at all . The overarching problem in this setting is that the audience arguably cannot mourn ill-defined victims with any sense of authority. Who is to be mourned? In what ways? To offer "thoughts and prayers" for a loss following a tragedy, either in person (see, for example, Goodhead [2010]) or online (see, for example, Marwick and Ellison [2012]), to leave flowers at the site of the attacks—these gestures may hold meaning to some but they strike me in critical/cultural terms as being embedded with the same sense of false completion that Hall attaches to media power in reportage. When children die in school shootings we must speak their names and tell their narrative truths, through their words and through the words of those who knew them best. Such journalistic practice not only honors their lives and memory, but amplifies their innocence and vulnerability, as some of the youngest to find significance in our history.

The guiding charge of critical theory is to ameliorate the human condition. To return to Poster's seminal assertion about critical theory, which I also underscored near the end of chapter 1: "Unlike some poststructuralist tendencies, critical theory springs from an assumption that we live amid a world of pain, that much can be done to alleviate that pain, and that theory has a crucial role to play in that process" (3). When we recognize and narrativize their innocence and vulnerability, we may begin to make sense of the value of human life in a way that allows us as a culture to prioritize new and ongoing conversations about bona fide freedom and security for children in our schools. We need to engage in the collective work of imagining the world they will leave for those who come after them. Our mediated immersion sometimes lulls us into basking in the pleasure of the moment. And there is value in that practice, from time to time. Our long view must be multigenerational to achieve robust and bona fide sustainability.

Let us conceptualize terra firma in thirty-year increments, planting, developing, cultivating, and protecting with the next generation as our guides. Journalists need to speak beyond themselves and audiences would do well to demand that they do that. As Poster articulated: "Words in our culture shamelessly point to themselves, like television newscasters who brashly admit their role in shaping the news, not simply reporting it" (1989, 10). The destabilizing force of gun violence in American culture, especially through school shootings like the one at Sandy Hook, is that it jars us away from our long-term aspirations into the trauma of the present. This trauma forces us to question what we think we know and how we might have been so wrong about long-held assumptions. We have sadly known for more than twenty years now, since Columbine, that schools are not always sanctuaries. Violent acts like Sandy Hook also force us to admit the fragile, malleable nature of childhood innocence. Clearer articulations of who the victims were—of their innocence and vulnerability—would help the audience understand them as individuals.

Clarity and visibility, with respect, deserve to become the order of the day, when reporting about school shootings like those that occurred at Sandy Hook. As Poster notes: "In this postmodern world the line between words and things, subject and object, inside and outside, humanity and nature, idea and matter becomes blurred and indistinct" (1989, 10) Fuller portraits of the victims would make evident the abject realities of the loss. In other words, children are not murdered in a vacuum: they have families, friends, community support. Failure to report about any of these bonds is to further strip the victims of any of the bonds that make us all human. Without the dialogues that bind us to each other, the human tapestries that unify us all, such reportage wrongly suggests that death happens largely in a void. All victims deserve multivocal reportage because it affirms their shared humanity. Children may be innocent and vulnerable, but their memory always deserves attention rather than to be narrated to false completion through operational fictions. We are devaluing the human experience when we do not tell stories that point to the magnitude of loss among us.

### Storying New Media Technology History

"Tangible reminders of the massacre still linger," begins a five-year retrospective article on the Sandy Hook shootings in the *New York Times*. The story continues: "On the door of the Blue Colony Diner, next to the quarter candy dispensers, a frayed sticker clings to the glass" (Rojas and Hussey 2017, par. 1). Communities like Newtown may never fully heal from the tragedies that made them part of the American imagination. Retrospective articles like this one tend to emphasize how the community is engaging in acts of remembrance. As journalists Rojas and Hussey write: "The displays of grief follow a familiar routine: Candlelight vigils and makeshift memorials. National offerings of thoughts and prayers. Pleas to tighten gun laws, immediately trailed by calls to avoid politicizing a tragedy" (par. 7). Retrospective articles emphasize, more than does the breaking news reportage studied in this case, the victims and their legacies. Consider the following evocative paragraph, which clearly recognizes and elevates the communitarian core of the tragedy: "The shock waves have, by now, faded to something more subtle. Yet they still ripple through the town, stirring concentric circles of anguish, leaving people with varying degrees of pain and differing sets of struggles. The victims' relatives are at the core. Beyond them are the teachers and students who witnessed the carnage and chaos that day; the police officers, emergency workers and doctors who responded to it; and then an entire community" (par. 11).

Such extensive narration about the victims, even five years after the fact, suggests that the Hallian trends about "operational fictions" (Hall, 1974, 23) identified in this case may be subsiding, at least somewhat. Through the "speed and reach" (Gurak 2003, 30) of the World Wide Web the names have reached me on a Saturday afternoon in South Carolina. Members of the media audience are able to connect, to remember. In this retrospective article, in fact, Rojas and Hussey list the names of the victims in the second-to-last paragraph of the extensive story, which spans more than forty paragraphs. Consider the value of naming: a name helps identify, recognize, and celebrate an individual being. Names are pleasurable to hold, too; we luxuriate in our monikers. Consider the beauty of those American sentences that begin with the affirmation *I am*. To be able to assign a name is to begin a hopeful journey toward the understanding of a person, place, thing, or difficult-to-quantify concept. Names constitute the initial blueprint for all that is to be eventually built, whether or not the process of building is ever completed. The name makes space for a conversation to emerge, and so it is to be prized as a first principle of being. Naming is the window through which the rest of the world becomes a potential object of/for understanding. Naming also provides a refuge from the worry of being discarded along with other cultural debris that is unjustly othered before it can be thoroughly and actionably understood. To name is to be engaged in an ethic of care that works to make meaning, serve justly, and engage with a deep sense of mercy. In Posterian terms, I assert that to name is to begin "alleviat[ing] pain" (Poster 1989, 3). A small step but an important one: affirmation of individual life, respect and care through recognition.

## 3    Storying FDR

Autoethnography seeks to understand the relationship between self and society. Communication autoethnographer Rose Richards has written: "Through telling our stories, we make ourselves" (2013, 91). Narrative storytelling is vital to the autoethnographic tradition in communication research (see, for example, Ellis, Adams, and Bochner [2011]). Media autoethnography is an emerging area of communication research (see, for example, Boylorn [2008]; Fox [2014]; Uotinen [2014]; Johnson [2014)]; Manning and Adams [2015]), and this book benefits from earlier bridging between these two areas. As media become entrenched in everyday life, we are increasingly living with and living through our mediated interactions. Specifically, in our digital moment we are increasingly using media to (1) influence, (2) shape, (3) reflect upon, and (4) reinforce our stories. In this book I propose these four stages of media autoethnography to lend insight into the relationship between self and society in our networked world. This book asserts autoethnography as a methodological lens through which to understand the narrative paradigm in communication research. As American adults incorporate social media use into their news consumption while continuing to embrace the internet, the media world more fully bonds to (and binds with) technologies, platforms, and devices.

Recognizing the inextricable place of media within the human experience, the time is ripe to use media autoethnography as a methodological lens through which to extend the narrative paradigm in communication research. This book in general, and this chapter in particular, looks to build in that direction. People have long made sense of their world through stories. Using the example of spectatorship in different contexts—including Mickey Mantle's death on television, watching Gene Larkin's pinch hit in the 1991 World Series on YouTube, and watching *Draft Day* on film—I employ the autoethnographic tradition in communication research to demonstrate the blurring boundaries between media and memory in our connected era.

Specifically, in this study I use autoethnography to assert that, in our digital moment, humans are increasingly using media to (1) influence, (2) shape, (3) reflect upon, and (4) reinforce their stories. My aim is to lend insight into the relationship between self and society in our networked world. Specifically, as narrative-driven, evocative, brief entities, which may be inspired by travel or a sense of place. Autoethnography foregrounds lived experience in a way that places the self amid the social to reveal the relationship between the personal and the cultural in the communication world. Compactness is a guiding philosophy rather than a finite entity. As I think about compactness, I humbly lean on the words of autoethnographer Carol Rambo and her articulation of autoethnographic sketches. Rambo has written: "A sketch is an incomplete study, by definition. Information is left out or suggested, and the mind's eye is invited to fill in the details" (2007, 533). Media autoethnography emanates from a similar place, but the compact quality of the work invites both opportunities and restrictions. I hope this methodological lens inspires the writer (and reader) to engage in a dialogue about space in written communication. This turn toward compactness seems meaningful during a cultural moment in which communication has become especially brief, owing to social media immersion. I embrace this cultural moment as an opportunity to expand the conversation about the nature and trajectory of communication research.

Like compactness, stillness appears valuable within media autoethnography. Today stillness is a rare commodity. A noun in American English, the word still is defined as "deep silence and calm; stillness." As NBC's Tom Costello reported on April 17, 2007, one day after the Virginia Tech shootings: "Like none that have come before, this university generation was born into technology" (2007, 5:53:53–5:53:58). I research online memorial groups; stillness is elusive. I am thirty-six, more than a decade older than those "born into technology," yet stillness eludes me too. I turn to the following definition: "Autoethnographers look in (at themselves) and out (at the world) connecting the personal to the cultural" (Boylorn 2008, 413). Fusing the personal and the cultural is meaningful because the process ideally provides insight into each side of that relationship. On the personal side I have learned to prioritize my perseverance, and on the cultural side I have learned the importance of placing my body in manageable situations, making adjustments when necessary according to the constraints of my physical disability, cerebral palsy. The hardest thing for me to do is stand still, in one place. My quads are weak. So I find ways to limit having to do that; most often I ask for help, for a hand. It's not that I can't stand still in one place, I just can't do it for as long as I would like. It's a process, so I work, I sweat, and as I have explored autoethnographically in the past, I try to start every morning on the treadmill.

On that point, I am starting to succeed more than I fail. For me, exploring autoethnographically continues to be about embracing imperfection. I view this embrace as an opportunity for optimism. Recognizing existing challenges is, in my view, a way to feel grateful for all that is well, personally and culturally. Following Boylorn (2008), when I look in I am more fully able to look out, and vice versa. There is a personal-cultural dialogue at the core of the experience for me. Folk musician Ani DiFranco, one of my favorites, sings: "their eyes are all asking / are you in, or are you out / and i think, oh man, / what is this about?" (boyd 1995, 1). Applying those lyrics to the personal-cultural, I want to respond to both. The personal is cultural and the cultural is personal. The personal is many things, including home, and the cultural is also many things, including media. Those labels are porous, overlapping. In this inquiry I work through where they intersect as well as where they diverge.

Inspired, I author autoethnographic sketches. Each sketch is separated by an asterisk. Leaning into compactness, I write the autoethnographic sketches (Rambo 2007, 533) below:

> I went to school with people who were refugees from war-torn countries. They taught me more than I realized then. How the world is a scary place in certain geographies, and then in others, it's just not. Not in that way, at least. Each of these autoethnographic sketches is its own geography. I had a teacher who once told me I was lucky to have been born in the United States. And so was she, my teacher quickly added.

> I once told my father that the best thing about a globe (or it might have been a map, I can't recall) is how it shows us where we live and where we don't live. As I have written about in the past, I was born and raised in Rochester, Minnesota, USA, the son of Hungarian immigrants.

We are living through the wreckage of Stephen Glass and Jayson Blair and in picking up my pen an apology feels like the right kind of catalyst. I am sorry for anything I might misremember, but I am committed to the truth as I can recall it.

I could write forever about growing up, what was it that Flannery O'Connor said? I am not sure if a good man is hard to find or not, but I did my darndest to try to be one. I recount how in Chemistry, when everyone was stealing quiz answers, I didn't look.

Somewhere in Alaska, there was a natural disaster the other day. I heard about it on the news. The earthquake "originally listed as an 8.0 but was downgraded to 7.9" (*Los Angeles Times* 2014, 1). I wondered what that much movement would feel like.

YouTube has a memory; whatever lived once is available forever—I found videos of one of my childhood heroes, an Italian soccer player named Salvatore Schillaci. I can't say for sure whether I watched these games live on television, the ones featured in the videos, but seeing Schillaci on screen felt a bit like finding my way home.

Reflecting on these autoethnographic sketches, I am reminded of sociologist and autoethnographer Laurel Richardson's words expressing "*doubt* that any discourse has a privileged place, any method or theory a universal and general claim to authoritative knowledge" (1991, 173, emphasis in original). Indeed, claiming knowledge is a life's work, likely one to be completed after me by others. Instead, braiding together experiences may reveal some wisdom at their points of intersection. It is the shared points that seem most valuable. Their value embedded in the opportunity to create common frameworks for lived experiences, across time, space and place.

The purpose of this chapter is to present a Wendellian feminist theory of disability analysis of the case of CBS *This Morning*'s found footage of President Franklin Delano Roosevelt (FDR) "being pushed" in a wheelchair. Susan Wendell's vision of a feminist theory of disability is the most appropriate theoretical lens for this chapter because it works especially well for understanding how disabled people "experience the world" (1989,

104) and takes particular care to recognize the "structural" (104), "physical" (106) and "social" (106) components of that experience. Specifically, as Wendell writes, individuals "experience the world as structured for people who have no weaknesses" (104). Moreover, Wendell recognizes as a disabled person, "I have a particular standpoint determined in part by both my physical condition and my social situation" (106). This theory is instructive in two ways: (1) it recognizes the structural, physical, and social reality faced by disabled people, and (2) it helps make sense of how that reality gives rise to a power imbalance in a largely able-bodied world. Applying this Wendellian theoretical lens to CBS *This Morning*'s found footage of FDR "being pushed" in a wheelchair helps the audience make sense of how and why that news item was narrated. I conclude this chapter by suggesting ways in which mediated narration of individuals with a disability might more fully affirm their agency as individuals.

Robert E. Stake's model of an intrinsic case study (1994, 237) provides the methodological lens for this chapter. I am drawn to this methodological lens in this case "because, in all of its particularity and ordinariness, the case itself is of interest" (237). Narrating a twenty-four-second clip is an act of extreme brevity, even in our digital media age, and doing so on YouTube all the more so. Moreover, my recognition of my standpoint as a disabled person, with its Wendellian structural, physical, and social reality, adds to the remarkable quality of this case for me as a researcher. Accordingly, it seems fitting to pair Wendell's work toward a feminist theory of disability with Stake's intrinsic case study methodology to analyze this case. My thesis is that, viewed through a Wendellian theoretical lens, this case presents a reductive narrative of disability as something needing to be overcome. Accordingly, I call for fuller articulations of disability in lived experience and encourage journalists to provide a more invitational and multivocal alternative for the future.

### Case Narrative

This section features the case narrative of the CBS *This Morning*'s found footage of FDR "being pushed" in a wheelchair, taking care also to incorporate the context as needed to help the reader make sense of the reportage and its significance as mediated narration. I have separated the twenty-four-second case into the most prominent blocks of its mediated narration.

*0:01 "More than six decades"*

At 0:01, the camera fades in from black. The audience sees CBS *This Morning* reporter Gayle King in the studio with the backdrop of the studio set behind her. Over King's left shoulder is what appears to be the iconic CBS eye emblazoned in wood. The eye appears to be backlit in blue. Over her right shoulder there is what appears to be shelving (or a frame) that has multiple slots or cubbyholes to it. A cubbyhole on the bottom right behind King is also blue-backlit and it features a globe, which is discernible in dimly-lit profile. In the cubbyhole above the globe, there is a different backsplash, a rustic and weathered brick wall, which captures the viewer's eye for its stark contrast to the deep blue below it. In front of the rustic, weathered wall, there is a stack of four or five books, also dimly lit, just visible enough to be recognizable as books. Reading the set behind King, the layout of the studio set aims at a serious tone. King is wearing small hoop earrings, perhaps silver or gold. She is also wearing a necklace with a diamond pendant on it. The butterscotch dress she has on complements the soft yellow-and-black color palette of CBS graphics.

The banner graphic along the bottom third of the screen has three elements to it. From left to right, the first element is a thumbnail of the Golden Gate Bridge in San Francisco. A portion of the bridge is featured, but what is most evocative in the image is the yellow-orange San Francisco sky (either at sunrise or sunset). The viewer's eye is drawn to the color because it is well matched with the other colors in the graphic. Moving right on the banner graphic, the second element includes two items: an image and three lines of text. The image is a small, yellow CBS eye, and the first line of text says CBS. This first line of text appears in white immediately to the right of that small, yellow CBS eye image. Below the white CBS text, the words THIS and MORNING are written in prominent white, indicating the title of the program in easy-to-read lettering that is pleasing to the viewer's gaze. A double line, white and brown-orange, marks the edge of the second element in the banner graphic. The third element in the banner graphic shows title and subtitle. The title appears in large black letters placed inside a solid yellow box, and the subtitle as a solid white box featuring black letters. The title appears above the subtitle.

To indicate that the news report is moving from one story to the next, the title and subtitle are moving from the previous story to the next one. As a faint outline at 0:01 makes visible, the previous story was titled CRITICAL CONDITION, with the subtitle COUNTRY STAR RANDY TRAVIS GETS HEART DEVICE. The still-visible faint outline of the previous story featured in the third element of the banner graphic reminds the viewer of the pace of the news, shifting as it does from one story to the next. The faded title and subtitle gesture toward the upcoming shift. Ostensibly, the last story was about Randy Travis and the next story will be about something else, though the viewer is not yet told what that topic will be. Across all three of its elements (and especially the third one) the banner graphic establishes the setting for the viewer: this televised moment is a news report, a sequence of the news of the day. To the right of the banner graphic a transparent, off-white/gray small CBS eye creates a lower-right boundary for the viewer's eye, ostensibly teaching the viewer where on the screen to focus attention. Notably, the CBS eye is featured in three prominent places on the screen:

(1) The large gray eye over King's left shoulder, backlit in blue, (2) the small, solid yellow eye on the bottom left of the screen as part of the second element of the banner graphic, and (3) the transparent, off-white/gray, small CBS eye to the right of the banner graphic near the bottom-right edge of the screen. These instances of the CBS eye make the station's identity evident for the viewer. The CBS eye (in all three of its shown forms) is reinforced as a representation of the station. While the visual elements are central to the first second of the newscast, the words that King speaks to open the report serve to establish its historical nature. From 0:00 to 0:01, King begins speaking while the camera is still fading out from black into the studio scene described above. King states: "More than six decades" which strongly suggests the prominence of time, and change over time, in the upcoming news report.

### 0:02 *"after his death"*

From 0:01 into 0:02, the first and second elements of the banner graphic remain the same. Perhaps the most notable aspect of this moment in the case occurs within the third element of the banner graphic. The third element transitions fully away from the previous story and the title RARE FOOTAGE FOUND appears, above the subtitle VIDEO SHOWS

FDR IN WHEELCHAIR, which together indicate the content of the current story. The news value of this story is strongly suggested in the title and subtitle for at least four reasons. (1) The footage is characterized as rare, emphasizing the reason why the viewer should pay attention. In other words, they are about to see something unusual, so the act of looking is worth the viewer's time and attention. (2) The footage is characterized as found, emphasizing that there was a quest or journey related to its discovery, emphasizing yet another reason why the story merits the viewer's gaze. (3) The subtitle drills down to the content of the news story: VIDEO SHOWS FDR IN WHEELCHAIR, which strongly suggests the prominence of the story, because FDR was a commonly used abbreviation when referring to U.S. president Franklin Delano Roosevelt. (4) The last two words in the subtitle IN WHEELCHAIR serve to explain the rarity of this news story. As FDR scholar Matthew Pressman confirmed to *Time*: "It is true that mentions of Roosevelt's wheelchair in the press were extremely rare. Mostly, news coverage depicted him as someone who had courageously triumphed over polio. This was the image that FDR and his advisers wished to project, and they largely succeeded" ("Myth of Roosevelt's Wheelchair" 2013, 00:01:31–00:01:48). Accordingly, the last two words of the subtitle reinforce the first word of the title: the focus of this news story is rare. King speaks the following words from 0:01–0:02: "after his death," which provide still more context for this story: the viewer is now able to place the time period of "more than six decades" within a specific lifespan—more than six decades after FDR's death. One of the primary elements of the news story, when the newsworthy event occurred, is thus being established through King's words. Just as importantly, the mention of death matters in this context because even lay audiences understand death as a finite state within the human experience. The opportunity for news coverage to add new or largely unknown information about an individual's life "after his death" ostensibly heightens the rarity of this reportage. In fact, from 0:01 to 0:02, the third element of the banner graphic coupled with King's words work especially well in tandem to help explain the rarity of this news story.

*0:03 "we're getting our very first look"*

From 0:02–0:03, the first, second and third elements of the banner graphic remain the same. The head-and-shoulders shot of King speaking continues, and this visual continuity suggests that the news story has found its focus, which King will soon deliver to the viewer. Visual continuity is, in itself, a small way of helping the viewer make sense of the story, because the now-stabilized banner graphic reveals the content and context of the news item. King's words at 0:03 add communality as a news value, alongside rarity, when she states: "We're getting our very first look." This phrase is a well-chosen way to continue introducing the story, for two main reasons: (1) King does well to include the audience in the discovery, selecting the word "we're," ostensibly to emphasize the fact that news consumption is a pursuit that has shared value for journalist and audience, placing each entity within a meaningful dialogue as members of the same community. In this case in particular, because it was found by a nonjournalistic source (a scholar), the footage represents a discovery for journalist and audience, further emphasizing the relatively (perhaps even unusually) shared (common) position of each entity in this case. Moreover, (2) the words "getting our very first look," emphasize another news value: newness. Specifically, these words seemingly implore the audience to watch, because they have not seen this before. The use of the word *very* is wisely chosen here, because its use suggests the newness of this information to be a particular surprise. Put simply, while a first look might refer to any number of expected items (the arrival of a new season of cars, for example), the use of the word *very* suggests that the first look is unexpected. This word choice thus reinforces the relative newness of the information that is being shared with the viewing audience. While sometimes discouraged in language use, the employment of *very* as a so-called "intensifier" (Fink in Taylor 2008, par. 2) succeeds here because it helps "add suitable emphasis" (Taylor 2008, par. 9) to the story, to allow the audience understand the newness of this particular news item. Employing *very* at this moment positions the viewer to more easily make sense of the story.

### 0:04 "at President Franklin Roosevelt"

At 0:04 the very first look is revealed as the camera cuts to an image of a man ostensibly being wheeled from one place to another. Cutting away from the studio is a significant event because it suggests there is something more important than the journalist to share with the audience, and that more important thing will come next on screen. Cutting is a visual representation of the newness that was foreshadowed with the use of the word *very* in the previous second. Cut to the new black-and-white film footage that appears on the screen. This footage, now displayed on the entire screen, is taken at a distance, and there is a line of individuals who appear to be military service members standing in front of where the wheeling appears to be taking place. Their standing appears important, as if to signify recognitions of an arriving dignitary (though those standing are not visibly saluting or at attention, as might traditionally be expected in such a case). Admittedly, it is unclear (at least to me) whether wheeling is occurring at all. Wheeling seems likely based on the banner image title and subtitle, but the only thing about which I am clear is that movement is taking place.

It is also unclear where the individual being wheeled is coming from or going to. Place-related details are not evident in the film footage, and King does not reveal place-related details in the narration. King's words at this moment are vital, though, because she reveals the individual being wheeled: President Franklin Roosevelt. At this moment King affirms her journalistic role of informing the audience about who is at the center of the news story. Thus, the central figure of the news story has been formally introduced to the viewer. Though we cannot yet clearly see him on film, we can trust he is there because the journalist, Gayle King, has informed us of his presence. Importantly, the power dynamic between journalist as audience has changed from 0:03 to 0:04. While the two entities were on a shared footing at 0:03 because of the newness of the footage, the journalist is now informing the audience about the subject shown on film. The journalist serves the audience—and the audience needs the journalist—in a more pronounced way than they did one second earlier. For providing the missing information, not only on-screen but now in spoken language, King is upholding the journalistic ideal of working diligently to inform the public about the significance of information that may otherwise be unclear to them.

### 0:05 "being pushed"

At 0:05 King is describing the scene that is unfolding in the black-and-white footage. Being pushed is the action being experienced by Roosevelt. The visual elements of the footage itself are difficult to discern, but because there is movement one might infer that the wheelchair is being pushed from one place to another. The strongest attribute of this second of coverage, its value to the journalist and the audience, may be that it helps visualize what it looks like to be transported, (ostensibly in a wheelchair). Representing wheelchair transportation—"being pushed"—in media is valuable because it is fairly unusual to see everyday life of a disability as mediated representation. In this moment, being pushed rises to the level of media coverage because of the person seated in the chair: the president of the United States. Being pushed emphasizes the stark paradox of a man in a position of great power unable to transport himself. Indeed, human vulnerability is emphasized through King's word choice at this moment in the footage. It is worth noting that other media outlets utilized the same phrase, "being pushed," when reporting the discovery of this footage. On YouTube, *Time* uploaded what appears to be ABC *News* reportage of this same film clip, for example, in which an unnamed anchor states: "He's being pushed in his wheelchair back at Pearl Harbor back in 1944" (00:00:00–00:00:04). The repetition of the phrase "being pushed" across the CBS *This Morning* clip and also the *Time* clip suggests that "being pushed" may be emerging as a way of discussing the act of transporting FDR in a wheelchair. Repeating this language, of course, also reinforces a limitations-of-movement theme, when referring to one of the most powerful politicians in the world at the time. Importantly, the *Time* uploaded clip provides two meaningful context items that are not included in the CBS *This Morning* clip: time and place. The viewer learns that the clip was filmed in 1944 at Pearl Harbor. The ability to assess time and place would have allowed the CBS *This Morning* viewer to more fully make sense of the event, but that information was either unavailable for or omitted from the CBS *This Morning* news story; the precise reason for its absence is unclear to me.

### 0:07 "in a wheelchair"

From 0:06–0:07, the film footage cuts again to a shot of three men (who are not identified in image or spoken language) seated (apparently on a bench of sorts, though the exact location is still unclear) and ostensibly engaged in conversation. King does not indicate who the men are (though one of them is almost certainly FDR) or what they might be discussing. This lack of contextual information is perhaps not surprising, though, because the story is focused on FDR being in a wheelchair, rather than on the content of their conversation. The cut from the moving wheelchair (of the previous few seconds) to the seated conversation of this moment in the case suggests that FDR arrived at his destination. In other words, the seated conversation is the outcome; the conversation can take place, as a result of having been pushed in the wheelchair.

*0:08–0:24 The Remainder of the Found Footage*

"This is an interesting story because it's something that the public never saw throughout his life. This film, only eight seconds long, was found in the National Archives by a professor from Franklin College, which by the way, was actually named for Benjamin Franklin, and not FDR."

The remaining sixteen seconds of the CBS *This Morning* attempts to underscore the news value of this news story but, as I argue below, presents a justification for its airing only to undercut that justification with an unrelated remark at the conclusion of the story. As the visual remains largely focused on the seated conversation, Gayle King uses spoken language to underscore news value. King says: This is an interesting story, which sounds almost like an apology to the viewer, a response to an unasked question—why play a brief clip of the president in a wheelchair on the air?—that is then answered in the next breath: because it's something that the public never saw throughout his life, reinforcing both rarity and death (specifically, new knowledge about FDR's life that has emerged after his death) as being at the core of the news value of this story. King then concludes the news clip with information about the clip itself. Importantly, King is seemingly justifying the brevity of the news report by explaining the brevity of the footage itself—"this film, only eight seconds long." King then mentions location information "was found in the National Archives" and source information "by a professor from Franklin College" before concluding the news report with an unrelated remark: "which by the way, was actually named for Benjamin Franklin, and not FDR." The remark suggests that King is working to keep the overall mood of the reporting light rather than serious in tone. One might suggest that the public likely wonders if Franklin College is named for FDR and so the remark might be justified in terms of news value.

What worries me, though, is that the unrelated remark (whether a joke or a serious attempt to inform the public) comes at the end of a sixteen-second stretch in which King appears to be speaking in an attempt to justify reporting the story. Importantly, the unrelated remark seems to undercut that justification process, diminishing the story's overall impact. Put simply, the first seven seconds of the reportage gives voice to a major figure in history and politics who thrived while also using a wheelchair to get around in the world. The remaining sixteen seconds, however, appear to be largely filler; the viewer never again sees journalist King, and there appear to be three visuals to fill out the report: (1) the conversation in the film footage is shown to continue, (2) there appears to be at least one closeup in the film footage (ostensibly of FDR, but no identifying information is provided in voice or image), and (3) there appears what looks like a repeat shot of a wheelchair being pushed. I wonder if the third shot is a repeat shot because it looks strikingly similar to the footage presented around 0:04. With neither confirmation nor denial in voice or image, it is impossible to know for certain if this is a repeat shot meant simply to fill out twenty-four seconds, or if this is a new, similar shot meant to close out the news report.

With limited visual context of any kind provided for the final sixteen seconds of the clip and limited meaningful spoken content in the final sixteen seconds by journalist King, the segment from 0:08 to 0:24 in the news report leaves important questions unanswered and forces the viewer into speculation rather than providing meaningful, necessary information. It is quite possible that the visual remains focused on the conversation because CBS *This Morning* wished to show the entirety of the eight-second FDR wheelchair film clip, but journalist King neither affirms that the conversation being shown is the full eight seconds of the National Archives clip, nor denies it. King simply states the spoken language, concluding with the unrelated remark, which may even be a joke. I infer that the conversation being shown at 0:08–0:24 includes the balance of the eight-second clip, because the tagline NATIONAL ARCHIVES appears in the top-left corner of the film footage at this moment in the case. But the precise origin and source of the film footage on screen between 0:08–0:24 is neither confirmed nor denied using visuals or spoken language in the report.

Thus, the portion of the news report from 0:08 to 0:24 arguably represents a missed opportunity in two ways: 1) the need to infer the source of the visual (likely though it may be) has potential to leave at least some audience members confused about what they are viewing and why it is being shown to them; and 2) the relatively less substantial and perhaps even joking tone of the last sixteen seconds squanders an opportunity for meaningful dialogue about the role of disability in history and politics. This missed opportunity is all the more unfortunate because the first seven seconds of the report offer a promising direction for such potential dialogue.

In sum, neither that promising direction nor that potential dialogue is ultimately realized. In Wendellian terms, the mediated narration in this case narrative strongly suggests disability as something to be overcome. In this reductive narrative of the disabled body, FDR is "situated" as though he is beholden to the nameless person who is pushing him, as he is "being pushed." He is accordingly "personally" stigmatized as someone who is unable to be an agent of his own moving and he is "socially" reliant on others to "be pushed." Recognizing critical theory as the seat of power through which to challenge the existing oppressive and reductive notion of disability as something needing to be overcome, I offer four admissions toward positioning a body for strength in a pluralistic world.

## Positioning a Body toward Strength

### The Body as a Source of Pain

The core of a strong body also is up for rearticulation because known avenues of/for likely heights suggests the body/ies would benefit from being remeasured to gain a fuller sense of their emerging depths. Foremost among these is the need to admit the body as a source of pain. As Wendell writes: "People with painful disabilities can teach us about pain because they can't avoid it and have had to learn how to face it and live with it" (1989, 115). In this section I work to position the body toward strength in a pluralistic world. Leaning into the reality of pain is a prerequisite for strength. In other words, acknowledgment of pain is required to place the body toward strength through poststructuralist ways of knowing. Placement provides an opportunity for altruistic ordering in a way that benefits rather than confines those stakeholders most directly impacted throughout the process. I aim to gather fragile quantities of consideration into discernible units of analysis as a sort of reconciliation against the reductive formations of earlier eras. A body can be considerably more than we imagine it to be—seated or standing, rising or falling. The falling body, in fact, is an opportunity to make sense of descending space in this context, explaining how gravity always demonstrates its spatial authority and how afterward there remain on the body remnants of the existing psychic hierarchies of the world at large. Accordingly, the first step in the process is to acknowledge the body as a source of pain, in critical/cultural terms. Returning to Mark Poster: "Unlike some poststructuralist tendencies, critical theory springs from an assumption that we live amid a world of pain, that much can be done to alleviate that pain, and that theory has a crucial role to play in that process" (1989, 3).

### Western Media's Power Over Narration of the Body

Having theoretical guises for the massive fluidity of the cultural experience provides one with enough of a jovial framework to build rather than excavate: episodes of concrete action are flashes of insight for the benefit of making sense of corporeal realms. Wendell rightly calls for cultural embrace and knowledge building on "what it is like to be 'too far' from the cultural ideal of the body" (1989, 115). These ways of knowing may take the shape of form or content, of news or entertainment programming. Ultimately, the body is always on the block of promises waiting to be vindicated in one way or another, owing to the fact that bodies and their knowing (as much as can be known) are often misunderstood or maligned. Camus, for his part, would note the body as missing or, at the more likely trajectory, losing what has struck it into meaning by the end of earthly life. Existential considerations are always fleeting and finite. Different stages of life (birth, youth, the working years, the period of retirement) carry specific opportunities and challenges of and for the body. Initial glances of admiration do not meet with affirmation into or toward permanence. To once again employ Denzin on representation and control: "Those who control the media control a society's discourses about itself" (1996, 319). There is indeed a Western way of knowing about liberation as an always-evolving goal that can never fully be reached or struck into being, because it is always under inquiry, most often conveyed through mediated narration. A completely free body will never bask in its own glow: constraints will always keep a body from total emancipation even if those constraints exist merely to insure its basic protection. Consider the dividing line down the center of a two-lane highway: that invention alone has saved more lives than are quantifiable. And yet the automobile as Western practice does and has transported more freedom than the human condition can reasonably encapsulate within the pages of this book.

## The Limitations of the Mediated Body

Mediation has yet to be an emancipatory force for/on the bodies that it mediates. Indeed, the mediated body admits only those constraints absolutely necessary for forward progress, perhaps some economic and social barriers intended to make the work of breathing the same air a workable exchange. The mediated body is usually strong and youthful. With intentionality, the youth tends to reinforce the strength and the strength tends to reinforce the youth: one often feeds the other in a seemingly infinite cycle. A mostly free body basks in some freedoms but ultimately finds itself yearning for what it does not possess or has not conquered. The ideal body, and the disabled body as counter to that ideal, has permeated media culture. As Wendell counsels: "Perhaps we could give up our idealizations and relax our desire for control of the body; until we do, we maintain them at the expense of disabled people and at the expense of our ability to love our own real bodies" (1989, 116). Derrida would, I gather, question the existence of this potential to "give up" anything altogether, wondering whether an edge has ways of making itself known through any sort of viable performance.

Braiding Derrida into Wendell, I wonder about the center of the body-as-structure. As Derrida writes: "As center, it is the point at which the substitution of contents, elements or terms is no longer possible" (1978, 279). The question at the core of my inquiry here is: what does a body need to be a body? I am asking in sociocultural terms, building from the underlying assumption that cultural bodies are sanctioned in and through media in specific ways and for particular reasons. The evidence adduced in this inquiry strongly suggests that certain bodies rise to mediated narration, especially those that evoke an appealing sense of stardom (athletes like Mantle and Larkin) or disgust (Lanza), but also that give rise to curiosity for their relative unusualness (FDR in a wheelchair). This evidence also helps answer the question I posed: a body seems to need a memorable, quickly discernable and, most importantly, easily visualizable characteristic to rise to prominence in mediated narration.

## Table 1. Certain bodies rise to mediated narration

| Quality evoked in mediated narration | Subject of mediated narration |
| --- | --- |
| Appealing stardom | Mantle; Larkin |
| Disgust | Lanza |
| Curiosity owing to relative unusualness | FDR |

This need is, of course, in tension with the fact that the cultural body is always permeable and porous, submerged against the corporeal reality, that though conditions may never be entirely favorable for its liberatory development, a body can and should look and perhaps lean forward against sociocultural and economic driving forces, working to articulate its emancipatory character. I return here to McLuhan's assertion: "It is the medium that shapes and controls the scale and form of human interaction and association" (1994, 9). Corporeal struggles would ostensibly tire most audiences, owing to their enduring narrative binds, in the way that repetitions of worn articulations of freedom and security provide little new: mediated narration tends to lean into what is known (for better or for worse) and to elevate what is most easily visualizable. Recognizable visuals are ostensibly sources of comfort (for example, Mantle as hero reads as true in the American popular imagination). Broadly accepted representations such as these might pacify, at least on a surface level, certain audiences. But at the end of the day the nonathletic body is still underrepresented. Audiences reading the mediated body through a Wendellian lens will rightly demand more diverse, pluralistic representations. McLuhanesque readings of corporeal struggles will also highlight the essential permanence of these struggles, and such readings will lead us into ways of exploring the inherent theories of electric light as a brightener, and technological dark as a dimming agent, in our American cultural moment. Corporeal struggles affirm that absence away from and outside of the technological present is difficult to master. With smartphones and tablets at the ready, we find it difficult to rest amid their volleys for our collective attention during this evolving epoch. We are living with and through our technologies alongside and within and upon our bodies.

*Pluralistic Representations of the Mediated Body*

Like cultural cowboys seeking a vast prairie but without a workable path on which to roam for the journey, those bodies find that hierarchies of meaning are distant indicators (like lighthouses to a vessel adrift in the water) rather than firm guides. The mediated representation of the cultural body is too often unforgiving, lacking any footholds on which the body might lean to gather its bearings. So mediated bodies are occasionally swaying, surveying what there is to reach for and how the essential material, in the form of pluralistic representation(s), may be obtained and secured. Each of these four admissions reflects a flag in the night, with its own desired and desirable elements, qualities, and considerations. More malleable than one would like to admit, each represents a way toward inquiry rather than a definite and fully knowable entity. Like the body itself the edge is teachable, training for a future that may or may not emerge, but in case it does arrive the trials and preparations of the body will serve it well.

Emancipatory bodies flourish where more constrained bodies falter. Wendell would likely classify the found FDR footage and the mediated narration in this case as evidence of a "disabled hero" (1989, 116). On this category of disabled people, she writes: "Disabled heroes are people with visible disabilities who receive public attention because they accomplish things that are unusual even for the able-bodied" (116). We as scholars and students and lovers of journalism must not succumb to the banality of the same bodies on the same screens, over and over again. It will certainly be a challenge, because what is required is to represent what the problem is and to also offer a solution to that problem. In this study the problem with Mantle as such is not Mantle, but only Mantle. The problem with Sandy Hook is easy visualization of a deeper crisis. The problem with FDR is the body as the defining and constricting element of the man.

In American media culture we need to reposition dialogues about strength to emphasize more pluralistic conceptions of what it means to be strong. Everything is considered a contest, a conquest, a zero-sum activity for the production and consumption of the mediated masses. This shortsighted consideration of cultural participation ultimately reduces the human condition to a series of doings rather than a set of malleable

### Table 2. Toward an expanded conception of strength

| Political | Economic | Social | Spiritual | Corporeal |
|---|---|---|---|---|
| Living in an open political society (freedom of movement, freedom of expression) | Enough resources to cover basic needs (food, water, shelter, clothing, utilities) | A strong social support network (friends, family, community members, colleagues, online or offline networks) | Ability to worship, believe, or practice (or the ability to abstain from it), as desired | Ability to use physical body to engage in movement as desired (to walk, to run, to jump) |

and fluid experiences. Critical theory has a vital role to play in this process. To once again invoke Mark Poster's seminal quotation about critical theory: "Unlike some poststructuralist tendencies, critical theory springs from an assumption that we live amid a world of pain, that much can be done to alleviate that pain, and that theory has a crucial role to play in that process" (1989, 3).

Notably, strength has political, economic, social, spiritual and corporeal components. While mediated narration tends to focus on the corporeal elements of this concept, doing so causes pain to those who do not reach that ideal. The pain may be Posterian "pain" (Poster 1989, 3) related to the difficulty of critical inquiry, or it may be physical pain, owing to its actual physical impact on the body itself. There is a need to point to the realities of strength as a multifaceted undertaking. To be strong is to have the capacity to define in each of these five ways the path of/for/ through progress and toward a more multivocal, ongoing conversation about those bodies that tend to dominate mediated narration in corporeal terms. A fuller selection of corporeal realities would rightly weaken this dominant, reductive narrative and provide a more invitational, multivocal alternative for the future.

In the process of mediated narration, the body becomes a contentious space. To reinvoke Denzin on representation and control: "Those who control the media control a society's discourses about itself" (1996, 319). Mantlesque bodies can do things other bodies cannot, yet they provide the standard other bodies are judged upon. Yesterday's understandings of given parameters are in everlasting dialogue with new frameworks for undoing previous representations of the body across a broad spectrum of stakeholders. Like a westerly migration of and for nodes of information, critical/cultural scholars must position their inquiries to make sense of a reconfigured landscape. In this book I aim to contribute to that area of consideration. Obtuse markings about the distinctions between mediated bodies are no longer necessary or instructive as audiences work to consider demarcation lines between modes of practice. What is needed is a return to the first principles of the undertaking—transparency and narrative growth—in the way that stories build their own extremities once they are given spatial and temporal outlets for breathing. To holistically make sense of the body and its knowing, critical/cultural critics must resist the easy if seductive allure of sensemaking in this overly concrete and positivistic direction. Scholars working in this realm must embrace not only Bochnerian doubt but also a Camusian sense that amidst the finite boundaries of corporeal pleasure there is much to examine, bring to the table of deliberation, and unpack for its essential and lasting essence. In doing so, we can work collectively to invite the body to a fuller consideration of/for mediated narration in the digital age.

The corporeal reality of the body will need to be more malleable and an agent of its own definition. Scholars tend to engage in their work with a sense of finite progress, and to an extent that work makes logical meanings. The problem of course is that not all the world can be engaged nor understood solely through the work of logicians. Much of the body is edging into an area that is either yet unknown or in some way difficult to grasp. To engage in corporeal considerations with a sense of mercy is to recognize the present limits of human understanding and press on all the same. The pursuit is a noble and meaningful effort even if it cannot be fully or easily digested in a single sitting. Multivalent readings and considerations, just as multivocal perspectives, often require the desire to return and reengage across spatial and temporal boundaries. To consider the body with a sense of mercy is to be engaged in an enduring, even decades or generations long, pursuit of deeper truths and more underlying, concrete, definable and discernible meanings. Past precedents must not be allowed to reign as constricted models for showing and telling the media world. Enduring pasts are valuable entities and they must be layered onto the everyday that lurches forward despite and because of all of its foibles. We must together as journalists and journalism scholars do the complicated work of "escaping the trap or [sic] objectivist naivete" (Derrida 1978, 34) that, if I understand his words correctly, threatens to bind concepts to their existent past(s). In this book, I have worked to do that. To narrate the body in a more pluralistic way is to plan for the future.

## Implications for the Future

The process of making significant strides in this effort is likely a generations-long endeavor. This complex work is further troubled by a lack of representational examples that would serve to counterbalance that/those past(s). May our stories always be interpretive collages of the worlds that we simultaneously inhabit and wish to escape from, toward something more robust and meaningful. Traveling through the no-longer-existent yesterday into something like the promise of the future, the feeble reality is that we have only this day, which I consider today but also to-day because it is the day to do what we can to move forward through media theory. I read the present as a call to action because it anchors reality to space, time, and place. Our shared work as scholars is a commitment to a sort of sensemaking that will outlive us on its path to fruition. We must as scholars be satisfied with doing steps along the way rather than engaging in a full dance card.

This level of humility (and recognition of it) does not necessarily come easily to a professional group that knows well the benefits of measurable progress. The progress we make may (and we hope will) be measured by those who emerge generations after we do. Embracing the profound discomfort of our almost certainly never-to-be-finished-by-us work will confirm the enduring value of scholarly engagement with production, consumption, and deliberation, We need also to embrace the struggle that is looking toward such a lofty enterprise. Re-presenting bodies calls us to re-name, re-prioritize, re-publicize and re-mediate, not unlike the way a painter paints over an existing canvas and creates an even better work. I am seated next to Larry Eigner and others as I work to transform conceptualizations of the value of the disabled body, and the measure of a body, disabled or athletic. I can only hope that I produce a meaningful mile-marker on the long road. A journey indeed, and one that I hope others will take up after me.

There is, as Derrida rightly noted, a "terrifying form of monstrosity" (1978, 293), and I take this conceptualization to foreground existential worry. Mediated representations of certain sort of bodies (mostly athletic ones) may compound the flaws of other bodies. A body without mediated representation risks gradual erasure or blurring out of the public consciousness. A mind bent in new directions struggles to map the resultant angle, and so it is a bit like traversing underground tunnels at a sensory deficit. The work is pleasurable only inasmuch as one is able to survive its telling: the slog on the way may well be arduous at least and intractable in more profound conundrums. We begin as scholars recognizing that we may not succeed, even if others may be more capable than we are. We begin with our skillsets in mind and then aim to establish what our bodies and hearts and minds and communities open along the way for us. Journalists have an opportunity to lead in this opening because of the power of mediated narration as a sociocultural force. If they do not lead in their reportage, it seems unlikely to me that nonathletic, nonheralded bodies will be able to make a considerable amount of cultural headway. The impact of the media star across the last century, and even the impact of the media influencer over the last five years, is simply too alluring to producers and consumers for them to make enough space for bodies that do not conform to this cherubic ideal. Failure, even more pressingly, does not look like anything damaging or dangerous. Rather, failure in this pursuit looks deceptively normal, the ostensibly placid conveyor belt of more-of-the-same.

## Storying the Body in New Media Technology History

As this study makes evident, disability is often reductively narrated as something needing to be overcome. The personal-cultural struggle inherent in these sentences reveals the ephemeral, fleeting nature of power and control when bodies do not exist inside already-established sociocultural norms. Bodies that cannot pass for "normal" (however we interpret that word) often position themselves toward it and hope for a culturally favorable reading. Although this binding of positioning and wanting is not entirely uncontrolled, those who have extensive tremors or spastic muscle movements (like me) worry about whether we will be allowed to participate in the broader arena alongside other bodies. Mediated narration is clearly in need of more complex representations, honoring the multivalent potentials of/for mediated narration. Mediated narration currently occurs in too simplistic a manner, one that does not fully capture either its potential or its problems.

Present-day mediated narration is therefore arguably unsatisfying to an audience. Underdrawing mediated narration, as I have asserted here, affords the audience limited opportunity to place themselves into a meaningful dialogue with the other(s). To reiterate, my thesis here is that, viewed through a Wendellian theoretical lens, this case presents a reductive narrative of disability as something needing to be overcome. Accordingly, I call for fuller articulations of disability in lived experience and encourage journalists to provide a more invitational and multivocal alternative for the future. There is a need to further research how/why/when narrations are messier than mediated representations would suggest and also how/why/when mediated representations might make room for narration other than those presented in these findings. Taking a more dialogic turn has potential to generate a fuller conversation about subjects, objects, and their knowing(s) across historical and present-day media moment(s). I hope the findings presented in this chapter inspire further critical media scholarship about the mediated body across space, place, and time. Constructing an understanding of the mediated body builds on critical media scholarship in a number of related areas, including mediated masculinity (see, for example, Lindgren and Lélièvre [2009]), media work as performance (see, for example, Coonfield and Huxford [2009]), the potential of/for online expression (see, for example, Crick [2009]), and YouTube as media platform (see, for example, Hess [2009]). Critical media scholars Lindgren and Lélièvre found that studying the MTV program *Jackass* "enables us to examine the problems and limitations of normative masculinity, and furthermore to explore possible 'other' male subjectivities" (2009, 409). Through emphasis on both Mantle and FDR, for example, I aim to contribute knowledge to what it means to mediate masculinity. The image of FDR in a wheelchair, in particular, has potential to open dialogue about how strength is mediated in the present-day communication environment.

# 4  Storying "Seven Days of Heroin"

Autoethnographically, I lean into community (see, for example, Ellis, Adams, and Bochner [2011]). The communities I serve: self into social and social into self, each feeding the other (see, for example, Reed-Danahay [2017]). I provide students with a strong foundation as writers, readers, speakers, and citizens in the digital media world, which will allow them to achieve employment in communication and related fields or pursue graduate study in the specialization of their choice. Across the curriculum I emphasize the dialogic nature of communication (see, for example, Denzin and Lincoln [1994]). Indeed, we are all always storying our worlds into being: we do it through the media we consume, the face-to-face conversations we have, and the experiences we share together. In our personal and professional lives, we are continually storying ourselves and others.

In the past, I have assigned students to produce and present a forty-eight-hour media+use journal. I grade student presentations based on their use of Aristotle's three intrinsic proofs (ethos, pathos, and logos) to persuade the audience they are living in a media world. Following Jay Blumler and Elihu Katz (1974), Anabel Quan-Haase (2008), Ralph E. Hanson (2018), and others, this assignment requires them to show a deeper appreciation for their status as active members of the media audience. A sophomore noted that they post on social media about their workouts using the MapMyRun app, as a way to visualize their progress and reach their goals. In Mass Media and Social Change, students author a final essay that asks them to employ the works we have read (from danah boyd, Neil Postman, Vaclav Havel, Bill McKibben, and others) to forecast the central elements of the media world twenty years into the future. Though some consider synthetic reflection a daunting task, others embrace it as an opportunity to examine the deeper significance of our increasingly mediated interactions with individuals and institutions.

A student noted the similarities between the call for democratization in Havel's *Open Letters* and the call for equity across race, class, and culture by Lauryn Hill in her album *The Miseducation of Lauryn Hill*, as a way to emphasize the importance of participation in closed and open political societies alike.

I set high standards for media production while providing a framework for success. When examining interpersonal communication in Media and Memory, for example, students produce an audio postcard to a friend or loved one, highlighting the significance of that person in their lives. I introduce the assignment with an explanation of the Sender-Message-Channel-Receiver (SMCR) Model (Shannon and Weaver 1964, 7), and ask students to be mindful of each element of the model in their audio postcard. Students often recognize how certain media privilege certain senses (for example, audio highlighting voice) in the human experience. A student expressed gratitude because the audio postcard allowed them to say goodbye to a loved one lost to suicide.

The resulting in-class discussions invite students to make sense of media-making as a path toward identity construction and a coping strategy against loneliness. During our reality television unit in Media History, I screen PBS's *An American Family* and MTV's *The Real World* before requiring students to produce a brief video response focused on a specific social issue they found compelling in either series. A student remarked that a telephone conversation between members of the Loud family was among the most boring moments ever aired on television and yet conceded the exchange was excruciatingly real in its depiction of everyday social interaction. Just as my research foregrounds my own positionality, my expectation for them is to reveal their hopes, worries, reservations, and aspirations about the networked world. When students write, read, speak and produce work, I require them to consider their position in relation to the text.

Students complete my classes with a firm understanding of how to be self-sufficient communicators on their own and when working in teams. They know how to engage the digital media environment using their own platforms, tools, and devices and can interact with specialists and lay audiences alike. These experiences allow them to chart their futures. Whatever changes may be ahead, they will be ready to respond and embark on the path that most closely represents their specific goals.

A few years ago my father went back to see the house in which he grew up, in Nyiregyhaza, Hungary. I asked him if he had any memories there, and he told me that he couldn't recall any specific thing, but that the house was nonetheless important to him as a starting point. My mother's childhood home, Jaszladany, Hungary, is memorable to me as an idea as well, because, to hear her tell it, she was in charge of catching chickens on the farm when it was time to eat. In their own ways my parents are each connected to the terra firma of their youth. I grew up speaking both English and Hungarian at home, and I carry this connection to land-as-starting-point in my own prehistory. My students, colleagues, and fellow humans each have their own prehistories and stories, too, and I work diligently to live and work in a way that invites their lived realities alongside my own as a rich tapestry of the human experience. In fact, I read silences as moments of prestory. I hope that dialogic educational strategies will reveal silences, and the conversations they lead to, as generative experiences in the communication classroom. I strive to remain open to learning, remembering Richardson's interpretation of Foucault: "Wherever truth is claimed, so is power" (1991, 173). Accordingly, I hope to be always walking toward truth, but it would not bother me one bit if I never definitively or with absolute certainty found it. The pursuit leaves one, and has left me, open to and curious for new information. The pursuit makes it possible for me to actively engage and scrutinize data around me. The pursuit ensures that the process is always ongoing.

As I have demonstrated in this book, I am a new media technology historian who employs case study research, autoethnography, and textual analysis to make sense of continuity and change throughout Western societies in the late twentieth and early twenty-first centuries. I work to place myself into dialogue(s) with the phenomena I study, equally fascinated by times of crisis and moments in everyday life. Whether the moments are of high or low intensity, I am eagerly on the lookout for how the layers of the everyday intersect to reveal how we might live better together. I focus on how technology has been braided into culture and what these braidings might mean for how we all work, play and live together. I employ mostly poststructuralist and existential theoretical orientations because time, space, and place seem to me to be extraordinarily slippery concepts, best examined in recognition of their positionalities and vulnerabilities.

I arrived at this approach because I know what it is like to be an outsider. Growing up with cerebral palsy, the son of Hungarian immigrants, I was outside of able-bodiedness while also being outside of linguistic norms. Being fundamentally different in each of these ways taught me to embrace the other, while also using my considerable socioeconomic privilege as the son of a surgeon to make space for everyone. In a way I have always been restorying my life, defying or redefining what is possible—I walk unaided and live independently, but cannot drive due to complications from my disability—and I therefore eagerly await, as I have written in the past, Elon Musk's self-driving car (truly!). The example of autoethnographers Art Bochner and Carolyn Ellis has taught me to write my story into my research, noting all of its twists and turns along the way. I am also incredibly grateful to a host of doctors, therapists, teachers, professors, coaches, mentors, family, and friends, who have embraced me on a journey toward finding my way. Collectively, these individuals have taught me (as I have written in the past) that although some people say I live with a disability, my disability lives with me. I thus embrace mind, body, and spirit as three lenses that help me see the world. I encourage all toward similarly introspective investigation of their own callings. The classroom is a laboratory for investigation. I invite students to arrive ready to embark on their own journeys. I feel fortunate to have the expertise and experience to be able to serve as their guide. Writing this book has allowed me to more fully make sense of my own communities and my participation within and among them.

Storying this book as a new media technology history, I have also found encouragement in Thomas de Zengotita's *Mediated* (2005) to unpack the broader cultural elements at work in the relationship between technology and society. To write about technology and the mind and body in 2021 is, foremost, an exercise in writing and thinking about multitasking and then, inevitably, about distraction. I write the word *ethnography* on the whiteboard with a dry-erase marker. As I work through the parts of the word with my Fall 2014 Scope and Methods students, we cycle through the details of the term as articulated by communication scholar Arthur Asa Berger in our textbook. Reflecting on that experience, I am reminded of autoethnographer Carolyn Ellis's writing on the board for her own students (2004, 1).

Inspired by Ellis, I realize that teaching often begins by writing a single word. In this chapter there are four threads of loose connection. The first three are teaching, learning, and exploring. The fourth thread concerns the act of writing itself. I am especially inspired by Laurel Richardson, who articulates so well the multiple threads in autoethnographic writing (2007, 1). I imagine these threads as a quilt in which each square speaks to the others in a distinct yet interconnected voice. In "'Sit with Your Legs Closed!' and Other Sayin's from My Childhood," autoethnographer Robin M. Boylorn asserts: "sayin's serve as lessons, warnings, instructions, compliments and advice" (2013, 175). I have long encouraged my students about the vital position of storytelling in mass communication. I encourage them to read mass media texts as stories, while also investigating the potential motivations of the storytellers and the specifics of the desired target audience. Put simply, stories have senders and receivers, each of which deserve considerable attention. In Spring 2015, my Media History students and I read autoethnographer Barbara J. Jago's "Postcards, Ghosts and Fathers" (1996) to examine a narrative family history. Placed alongside media historians such as James Carey, Michael Schudson, and David Nord, we discussed the many ways to tell a history.

In August 2013, my first week as a tenure-track assistant professor, I walked into a room where we will have an introductory faculty and student meeting. Student leaders are finishing up a meeting of their own, when one of them asks me if I am "a member of the bunny family"—a group of students—to which I reply something along the lines of, "Actually, no, I am a professor here." In the moment, I am sure I felt a bit stunned. Reflecting on the experience about two years later, I now consider the student's question as a compliment (though a surprising one) and a reminder to do what I can to stay young, to be intellectually curious, and to remain connected to my students. I am inspired by the prose poems of David Shumate and I work to unpack the nature of scale, in terms of what matters most as part of the human experience. The three autoethnographic sketches below articulate some of those connections:

1. I write toward some kind of light: My partner bought a flashlight, two of them, for our go bag. My home is strategically located near a nuclear reactor, and in the event we ever have to get up and go, I want to bring a pen and paper. Forget all of my stuff, I want to write. My mother's French teacher in high school was Miklos Radnoti's widow. Radnoti was a Hungarian poet, killed by the Nazis. When they dug up his body

to give him a proper burial, they found his last poem on his person. I'm not sure if it was in his pocket or what, but I heard they found his last poem and a small picture of his wife. I hope that is a true story, because I want so much for it to be true. People are people and stories are stories, everything else is just heavy. Learning is a process that works best with certain affordances, including a physical space in which my body feels connected to (and comfortable amidst) the physical surroundings.

2. I am sitting in the balcony during Welcome Week at the London School of Economics in Britain. It's early October 2006 and the usual first-week festivities are under way. We're being told what to expect, what to look for, and so on. I've got Ted Kooser's poetry, specifically his book *Delights & Shadows*, in mind as I remember that experience. I admire the way that Kooser writes about the everyday experiences associated with life in the Midwest. Kooser's poetry reminds me, still today: sometimes the only thing the heart needs in order to relax is just to look out the window and find the blue sky. Whenever I feel distant from my work, Kooser's words help center me. Concrete reflections on everyday life ground me in time, space, and place.

I have written about my experience in London in the past (Gloviczki 2016) and, as I note there, my experience in London lasted for a very short time. Taking inspiration from autoethnographer Tony E. Adams provides me with the opportunity to reflect on one of the happier moments from that time period, allowing me to more fully make sense of my time as a whole. Considering the tensions associated with new beginnings in journalistic work, I especially note the way that I work on "making the strange familiar" (Sikes 2013, 523) through the writing process as a professor and as the author of this book. And there is another thing, too. I have probably watched Michael Collings's first audition for *Britain's Got Talent*, his performance of "Fast Car," about a hundred times. The performance is available on YouTube and in it the audience meets a young man with a big voice. Michael looks (and acts) a bit young in the video and, to my read, he seems a bit uncomfortable in the spotlight. I like both his persona and his performance because they remind me of the underdog: someone who isn't expected to do well and then does. Collings has received millions of views and he has helped put the song "Fast Car" back on the music map. The underdog has made good. May journalists and journalism(s) always remain mindful of the underdog(s).

3. I read elements of my own story as one sort of underdog story as well. "The good Lord gave us two great things," he said, gesturing with a baseball bat toward his legs. Tom Carr was my batting instructor. While in school I attended batting lessons at the Rochester Athletic Club in Rochester, Minnesota. Rochester is a city of about 120,000 people in the southeastern corner of the state, and it is known for two things: medicine and IBM. The city is home to the main campus of Mayo Clinic.

I also note the pronounced influence of Judeo-Christian religion in American culture. That fact is probably the reason why I remember, about twenty years later, Mr. Carr's phrase "the good Lord." I did not take then, nor do I consider now, those words to be especially religious in his speech. He was simply expressing thanks for active use of his legs, especially within the context of swinging a baseball bat. As a researcher within online memorial groups, I have noted the use of Judeo-Christian expressions, including the use of the common phrase "God bless" or "prayers" during times of crisis. I read these words as first a collective expression of thought within a culture that is seeking to express support to the affected group of individuals. For those who are religious, the words may carry that level of meaning, though that level of nuance is not possible to discern through the study of the postings themselves. Additional research would be needed to determine the religiosity of individuals who post within online memorial groups. I read the above expressions as revealing the overarching American sentiment during tragedies, whether they are school shootings like Sandy Hook or the drug crisis in Ohio and Kentucky.

There is a historical consideration at play in this occasion, too. On December 11, 1968, NBC's John Chancellor reported about urban affairs. He focused on a game that was used in the planning of the city of the future. A computer was used to aid the process. Chancellor noted "the computer that is their partner and antagonist in the game" (1968, 00:03:50–00:04:10). Still today, the networked world seems to provide a host of affordances and constraints. To stay connected is to stay distracted, the distraction at certain times welcome and at others less so. Connect, disconnect, reconnect. A mantra, for computers as for communities.

## Understanding Christians's Theory of Authentic Disclosure

The purpose of this chapter is to present a Christiansian theory of authentic disclosure in news coverage in the case of the *Cincinnati Enquirer*'s

"Seven Days of Heroin" coverage. Clifford Christians's notion of authentic disclosure in news is the most appropriate theoretical lens for this chapter because it demonstrates the potential for mediated narration to more holistically narrate the experiences of underrepresented populations. As Christians writes: "A more sophisticated concept of news, consistent with dialogical ethics, is authentic disclosure. In this perspective, reporting must be grounded historically and biographically, so that complex cultures are represented adequately" (2007, 126). This theory is instructive in this chapter in two ways because it (1) recognizes the need for advances in news reportage and (2) prescribes a more holistic approach, "grounded historically and biographically" to work toward better "representation." Applying this Christiansian theory to the *Cincinnati Enquirer*'s "Seven Days of Heroin" coverage provides a more diverse, pluralistic model for the future of journalism and mass communication.

"I want to tell everybody in this room how proud I am of all of us and how proud I am of our ability to work together this way, but mostly I want everybody to know that we did this for the right reasons. We have a giant terrible, terrible thing happening to our community" (Wilson 2018, 00:00:13–00:00:29). These were the words of Amy Wilson, storytelling coach at the *Cincinnati Enquirer*, addressing the newsroom after receiving the word that "Seven Days of Heroin" had won the 2017 Pulitzer Prize for local reporting. Enter longform narrative journalism, with its capacity to unfold and reveal to and through and for the audience. As Ben Yagoda has written: "By stepping out from the shadows and laying bare his or her prejudices, anxieties or thought processes the reporter gives us something firmer and truer to hold onto as we come to our own conclusions" (1998, 16).

What matters most, then, is not the style or school of journalism (breaking news, narrative, literary, or some combination of all of those styles), but rather, the reportorial approach. The reporter's way of knowing the story as presented in fuller recognition of the reporter's position and the particulars of that position. In calling for a broader conception of journalism and in highlighting the need for Christiansian communitarian approaches, I am also reminded of geographer Stuart Aitken's claim that "violence, like youth, addiction and masculinity, is not a monolithic idea and can be viewed from different affective angles" (2012, 131). My findings in this chapter suggest that journalists should write, speak and document those "affective angles" into mediated narration. This view of the journalist as long-form narrator, in fact, also reminds me of the famous dictum attributed to sociologist Robert Ezra Park: "Go get the seat of your pants dirty in real research" (Kivisto 2017, 51). Telling the stories of these heroin addicts and of their community/ies seems to be grueling, engaged work. This sort of reportage is not only giving voice to the community's "pain" (Poster 1989, 3) but is also ideally helping addicts and their communities find a way forward apart from addiction. Never having been an addict myself, I hesitate to suggest that anyone can ever actually "be free" of addiction—it seems short-sighted based on my outsider's perspective—but it does seem possible that an addict might at least become estranged from the addiction, effectively structuring a life in which the addiction no longer governs everyday interactions. Journalism in a communitarian way seems close enough to the issue and its telling (laden with emotion as is such an enterprise) to make significant strides in that direction.

Analyzing "Seven Days of Heroin" in this chapter, I again utilize Robert E. Stake's intrinsic case study research methodology (1994, 236–37). The coverage warrants an intrinsic case study because it has been lauded as an exemplary moment for longform local reporting, an accolade which is especially noteworthy as brevity continues to be the order of the day on social networking sites like Twitter and Snapchat, among many others. I am asserting in this case that expansive, detailed journalism is worth exploring and understanding because it runs counter to the emerging cultural trend toward brevity in early 2020 in the Western world of journalism and mass communication. Because I have articulated intrinsic case study research methodology in earlier chapters, I will not repeat myself here. It is, however, worth noting the utility of an additional methodological tool in this case, because of the depth and breadth of the text, images, and video in the "Seven Days of Heroin" case. That methodological tool is textual analysis. Alan McKee notes: "When we perform textual analysis on a text, we make an educated guess at some of the most likely interpretations that might be made of that text" (2003, 1). Situated in American culture, immersed in this country's higher education tradition, and actively engaged in a liberal arts environment as an assistant professor of communication, I am reasonably well qualified to read the text in this case for its significance, especially as it relates to a way of knowing the communication world.

## Reportage Reveals Community Impact

"Seven Days of Heroin" especially captures the community impact of heroin use in Ohio and Kentucky. The *Enquirer* introduces it in the following way: "The Enquirer sent more than 60 reporters, photographers and videographers into their communities to chronicle an ordinary week in this extraordinary time" (*Cincinnati Enquirer* 2017, 1). Three themes from video reportage of this story emphasize the Christiansian approach taken in this case:

### Theme 1: Uncertainty from a Sibling (About If Living or Dead)

> 3:17 p.m. West Price Hill (Monday)
> "Hello?" "Hello! Cincinnati 911."
> "Yes, please, sir, my brother and his friend have overdosed."
> "Where you at?"
> "In the car, I'm by the Rapid Run Park, oh my god!" "Are they breathing?"
> "But what if they're blue?"
>
> (00:02:13–00:02:28)

### Theme 2: A Call for Help from a Friend

> 7:54 p.m. Newport, Kentucky (Monday) [indistinguishable noise]
> "My buddy, he's not answering his phone. I believe he's OD'ed (overdosed) and I think he's dead." (Brackets mine for clarity).
> "Can you tell me for sure if he has a pulse, or a heartbeat?" "Um, he's, aww, he's fuckin' cold"
>
> (00:02:29–00:02:40)

### Theme 3: A Mother's Grief

> Kim Hill, Mother of Thomas Burke:
> I got a phone call, she was all upset. I couldn't understand her at first. And I said: I think she's telling me my baby's dead.

No, it's not real, no. I don't know. It feels like your soul leaves
your body.

It felt like somebody just blasted me in the chest with a shotgun,
it's what it really felt like.

I guess they see it so much, they just look at it like, well, there's
another dumb ass, whatever. That coroner said I deal with
this every day. They come, well, we deal with this everyday.

I said: Yeah? Well, I don't deal with this every day. I don't deal
with—

I don't deal with it, I don't got to deal with it every day and bury
my child. Every day, my child's dead. I don't deal with that
every day.

How would you feel if you went home and your child was dead?

(00:02:41–00:03:20)

Taken together, these three video excerpts emphasize the binding together of the interpersonal impact of drug use and the community impact of drug use. Journalists are certainly working toward a more Christiansian "biography" of the drug problem in Cincinnati. Foregrounding these narratives places more pluralistic perspectives at the forefront of the reportage. Moreover, these three examples remind us that we must live in our power as communicators, always striving of/for/toward fairness and justice for those whose corporeal stories are not embedded with the same sort of privileges as our own contain in multitudes. Specifically, these three examples reveal a sibling, a friend, and a mother, respectively, working to story their beloveds' lives into a cultural narrative. Raising the overall level of discourse contains within it robust potential for a more equitable dialogic future. A representational plurality is possible if we engage together. Rewriting the corporeal narrative in American media culture is not most precisely rewriting. It is new writing in recognition of and reconciliation with the past. Running toward the pain rather than away from it. To underscore Mark Poster's articulation of the project of critical theory: "Unlike some poststructuralist tendencies, critical theory springs from an assumption that we live amid a world of pain, that much can be done to alleviate that pain, and that theory has a crucial role to play in that process" (1989, 3).

### Table 3. Characteristics of emotion in mediated narration

| Characteristic: relatable | Characteristic: universal | Characteristic: extraordinarily felt |
|---|---|---|
| Uncertainty (as in theme 1) | A call for help (as in theme 2) | Grief (as in theme 3) |

Carrying forward Poster's formulation, we must keep our records of the past close, honoring both what went right and what went wrong, riding on a spirit of free inquiry, leaning into the pain of the past in order to work toward "alleviat[ing]" (Poster 1989, 3) it in the future. Building the future must be an act of co-construction between journalist and audience, individual and community. To reiterate James Carey: "Cultural studies make up a vehicle that can alter our self-image" (2009, 94). Just as journalism would benefit from an updated "self-image" amid the technological reorientation under way in our digital age, so too would struggling communities in Ohio and Kentucky, and across the country. To build that updated "self-image" requires a renewed commitment to narrative storytelling that is centered in the history and memory at the core of the human experience. Foregrounding a sibling, a mother, and a friend, respectively, as the *Enquirer* has expertly done in the reportage excerpted above, suggests that some media organizations are making significant strides in this process. Notably, these three themes strongly suggest characteristics of emotion in mediated narration. Emotions must be relatable or universal or extraordinarily felt (or some combination of all three of those qualities) to be effectively storied into mediated narration. The uncertainty in theme one makes it particularly relatable, the call for help in theme two is especially universal, and the grief in theme three is extraordinarily felt.

Reporting the community's pain through vantage points such as these strongly suggests that the staff of the *Enquirer* rightly recognizes that citizens are the engine that will power the community on its journey away from ruin and back to renewal. As Art Bochner has suggested, journalists and audiences must participate in the human experience together and must honor our fallibilities and frailties, recognizing our doubts about our pasts, presents, and futures: "Memory is active, dynamic, and ever changing. As we grow older, or face unexpected traumas or disasters, our relationship to the events and people of the past changes" (2012,

161). I would also add that we must all do that for the sake of building a more authentic disclosure in the Christiansian way: working toward a fuller sense of the everyday reality. In this way, we must reveal pasts we would rather hide.

In narrative terms, succeeding at this process requires us to first engage in the dialogic act of listening. We do not as a culture know all of the answers, and we must admit our own shortcomings. When a sibling, a friend, and a mother speak as these do, and when their testimonies come forward as they do so boldly in the *Enquirer*'s reportage, we hear personal histories, lived biographies, in a way that destabilizes the existing power structure and opens representation to new and novel voices, voices of those touched by crisis who are otherwise, too often, undervoiced. This journalistic practice carries with it recognition of our poststructuralist moment: the human experience thus appears in mediated narration in a more robust, multivocal manner. To reiterate Christians's principle of authentic disclosure: "Reporting must be grounded historically and biographically, so that complex cultures are represented adequately" (Christians 2007, 126). The *Enquirer*'s reportage succeeds in these Christiansian terms because it skillfully braids together the interpersonal and the communitarian through individual histories and biographies. As these three excerpts strongly suggest, the personal thus becomes cultural, the individualistic represented as communitarian.

## The Promise of "Seven Days of Heroin"

The promise of "Seven Days of Heroin" is a more multivocal, more humane consideration of lived experience through longform local journalism. Building on these significant strides will not be simple. But if journalists engage the disabled and othered body as they are beginning to do (like the Pulitzer-Prize winning coverage noted herein), then there is a chance that a more detailed conceptualization of the human experience (for all of its positives and negatives) can be presented in the media world. Hearing the narratives of others, those who have traditionally not been present within the mediascape, is a vital step. Allowing them to narrate their own experiences will be doubly beneficial. And these narrators must be embraced as meaningful, viable, trusted bringers of meaningful information. Narration is a relational enterprise at its root and a community-sustaining enterprise at its best. Consider the relational power of sportswriter Bob Considine's declaration: "Listen to this, buddy, for it comes from a guy whose palms are still wet, whose throat is still dry, and whose jaw is still agape from the utter shock of watching Joe Louis knock out Max Schmeling" (1999, 138). The audience is drawn into the experience of the reportage: the result is extraordinarily felt, for journalist and audience alike. Considine's evocative details help the audience focus on the lived reality of the phenomenon he is experiencing.

We as scholars across communication and related disciplines must recognize the opportunity that awaits us as not simply a theoretical exercise but a way toward active, beneficial engagement with what lies ahead. Members of the media audience grow pleased by certain patterns as well: the stories that we feel are trustworthy and comfortable to read, hear, see, and listen to. The reality is that news stories are too often a reductive vehicle through which to breeze the news of the day into and back out of our consciousness without applying much consideration to their core elements. Reporting felt phenomena can help gradually re-engage our consciousness with specific details, evocative vignettes. We as a media audience must look even more closely and engage stories for the absences that are not stated as much as for the presences that are made apparent. Media organizations must acknowledge and embrace their power. Returning to Denzin on representation and control: "Those who control the media control a society's discourses about itself" (1996, 319). The crux of media literacy is to be mindful of the normative elements of the storytelling—what ought to be presented and where it ought to be presented. We as audience members should thus raise our expectations of media makers and exercise our right and obligation to respond when they do not meet those expectations. The call-and-response model afforded by social media platforms is only truly meaningful if it is engaged to its fullest extent by its users.

Social media researcher danah boyd touches astutely on the sense of forward progress inherent here: "The tensions between the technologies that help create networked publics and the publics that are created through networked technologies reveal how the nature of public-ness is actually being remade every day in people's lives" (2015, 205). Digital activity thus becomes part of our sleep-wake cycle, we move forward with and through our bodies, carrying with us whatever we can. We are all always public beings, as boyd suggests, and for members of struggling communities like those in Ohio and Kentucky dealing with the heroin epidemic this publicness contains the extra fatigue of evident otherness. Whether we choose to wear our otherness as a badge of honor or whether we shield ourselves as much as we can from public view, the political realities of everyday life today are, endorsing boyd's perspectives, also laden with both social and political consequences.

Working collectively, journalists, audiences, individuals, and communities must engage ourselves as those humans who are ready, willing, and able to trek down that path. The more numerous the membership in our illustrious club, the more likely we are to emerge from the struggle with at least modest victories. Concrete stories, such as those covered in "Seven Days of Heroin," are meaningful milestones along this arduous path. The clarity of a human story, with its beginnings, middles, and ends, winding though the path may be, is vital. Indeed, clarity is a helpful antidote to the inevitable confusion that accompanies uncomfortable work like community building. To return to critical theorist Mark Poster's wisdom about the intermittent chaos of our times: "In this postmodern world the line between words and things, subject and object, inside and outside, humanity and nature, idea and matter becomes blurred and indistinct" (1989, 10). Journalists and audiences would do well to embrace clarity when and how they can. The stories in "Seven Days of Heroin" provide a meaningful framework to employ in the future.

From a research and analysis perspective, measuring these victories and mapping them may prove easy in certain cases and more challenging in others, but our shared drive must be uniform and unwavering. Here, too, as I noted regarding new conceptions of potentials of the disabled body in chapter 3, broadening discourse is akin to a remodeling job; we must not be afraid to engage in the work of constructing new blueprints as useful. Fuller representation, at least on a macrolevel, of communities and their struggles, is a quantifiable and measurable activity that we must not shy away from throughout our efforts. Small modicums of progress can ultimately stack one atop the other to point a path forward, as does large evidence of progress. Learning to change happens at the incremental level, which is where we as students and scholars must affirm to begin. Before we finish the building, we must draw out the plans for the entryway.

Let us be intentional about our collective series of steps; let us step together for the benefit of carrying an entire community together. Joint work may be more labor intensive, but it undoubtedly increases the likelihood of lasting impact. Notably, such purposes must be acted upon in order to become fruitful. The work of mediating these concerns and bringing them into narrated conversation is specifically required. The mainstream dialogue must be expanded to include peripheral voices with a sense of fullness and nuance. Though emotional underpinnings may drive the effort, feelings alone cannot move the dialogue: the felt world must be driven to begin walking toward a stated goal. As Denzin and Lincoln have written about qualitative research itself, this process involves "a series of essential tensions, contradictions and hesitations" (1994, ix). If critical/cultural thinkers persist, the potential payoff is a multivocal, Christiansian reality that will make previous articulations of the body appear decidedly strange and unfashionable.

I noted in chapter 3 that journalists and audiences must admit and story the pain of disabled individuals; the pain of communities struggling with drug use, like those covered in "Seven Days of Heroin," must be both admitted and storied into the media world as well. Recognizing, of course, that common wisdom is often what has been layered so deeply into a culture that it cannot know itself without these rooted waypoints, I aspire along with my critical/cultural mentors (most notably in this context, Christians) to imagine a future wherein community struggles are recognized and boxed and mapped and measured as entities that are always open to interpretive development and ongoing critique. Constrained and confined communities are communities at risk. The work of mediated narration, and ultimately the work of critical media studies scholarship, is to continue issuing an invitation as a sort of reminder that communities never end, and what a sociocultural gift it is that our community-driven knowings might remain fresh, valuable, and enduring.

## Digital Implications for "Seven Days of Heroin"

The internet is a cartographic universe of ethereal connections. But the ethernet landscape is far away from the urban realities featured in this chapter. The distance created of/through digital spaces helps solidify the proxemics of urban troubles. The everyday transactional elements of landscapes suggest nominal consideration of what is occurring at hand. To return to geographer Stuart Aitken's perception: "Violence, like youth, addiction and masculinity, is not a monolithic idea and can be viewed from different affective angles" (2012, 131). What I mean to suggest is that consideration of urban challenges in journalistic reportage tends to be superficial at best. The reportage at the center of this chapter is notable for how it delves into the narrative arc of the affected individuals. The words in the article and the words and images in the video reportage construct the essential core of the lived experience. Language is expanding the audience's consideration of the human elements of the reportage.

It is worth reinvoking cultural theorist Stuart Hall's conception of operational fictions here. As Hall asserts: "Objectivity, like impartiality, is an operational fiction. All filming and editing is the manipulation of raw data—selectively perceived, interpreted, signified" (1974, 23). As I wrote in chapter 2, Hall is asserting that journalistic storytelling is an assemblage of meaning(s) strung together to tell a specific story. In the case of the heroin epidemic in Ohio and Kentucky, then, unearthing the corporeal humanity of each individual points toward the shared nature of the reportorial collective. Specific stories like those in "Seven Days of Heroin" represent the value of diligence to unearth the pain of bodies engaged in suffering. The scope of the suffering, in fact, spans not only those individuals whose bodies are directly engaging in harmful acts, including drug use, but also touches individuals whose bodies are geographically or emotionally in proximity. As these stories do so well to make evident, both the geographic (Aitken) and symbolic (Hall) reach of drug use is vast.

Untangling this reach and mapping it in a discernible manner is one of the overarching public service elements of investigative news stories like this one. Accordingly, it becomes more easily possible to plumb the depths of such social ills. The journalist provides an awareness-raising moment for audience(s), owing to reportorial work, and all the more so in the case of "Seven Days of Heroin," with its emphasis on familial and community impact. Reportage about drug use sheds needed light; hiding the problem does little to ameliorate it, although an absence of regular study may present the illusion that problems like drug use are improving, akin to closing one's eyes to the actual, ongoing truths. The truths are still present, even if one chooses not to see them. As a result the visual field (especially still and moving images) represents a particularly persuasive landscape for a reckoning with the challenges of substance-related dependence.

The narratives in "Seven Days of Heroin" suggest that addicts sometimes conceptualize the substances to which they are addicted as bringer(s) of hope amid an otherwise pitch-dark landscape. What I thus term as the silver-lining defense for abuse behaviors sheds needed light on one of the thematic psychic elements of destructive behavior. While individual narrative testimonies are neither necessarily representative nor generalizable, such narratives do focus on the heightened storying of stress and tension in this coverage. These articulations of stress and tension may affect journalists, editors, and readers alike, demonstrating that the enduring impact of coverage might reach beyond the addicts themselves. Reading the narratives in these pages thus becomes a mode of community-building, organizing the constellations of meaning in a vast trajectory outside of the reportorial field. Core emotions including fear and doubt are, according to the reportage, at the corporeal center of these addicts' overarching narrative worlds. The print, broadcast, and online elements of the media world are occasionally anchored within the tight boundaries of a specific medium, but increasingly cross-mediated considerations (a print story that also appears online) are becoming the order of the journalistic landscape.

Technology can constrain even as it expands, allowing audiences to cage themselves in a world emotionally distant from present-day realities. The vast archive of knowledge consumption in which online audiences sometimes confine themselves can disorient media consumers to the *veritas* of the day-to-day. What should ultimately be created in these landscapes is a brighter spatialization of the trajectories between dependence and independence.

A more humane media ecology in our digital age should consider how/when/if an individual's narrative arc is lingering closer to or further away from independence. Into Posterian "pain" (1989, 3) or away from it. Living toward human emancipation is a journey that includes a host of scholarly fields. In a poststructuralist tapestry, the slick holds of freedom or at least the absence of bondage are often elusive to grip. The ability to ameliorate one's independent condition thus represents one form of core innovation capital. Bringing one into a fuller corporeal state inside the able-bodied is a meaningful form of upward mobility. The outcome of this process affords an openness in the direction of representative potential. We in the media world need more representations of ability and disability, in order to understand the variety of paths through the human experience. Employing transparency as a guiding value, one might find considerable potential for restructuring the available catalogue of vocalizable experiences. Voicing those narratives breathes a sense of flexibility into the oft-limited ceiling of the media world. Transparent reportage has the potential to inspire a rewalling of mediated boundaries when reporting on corporeal elements of everyday life.

New media rhetoric calls on producers and consumers, journalists and audiences, to question the established corporeal understandings that have swept into media culture. Culture is often a slow-moving beast, assuming itself to be more comfortable with what is well understood than what is poorly understood. Even in our dynamic communication environment, the desire to challenge well-understood infrastructures is fairly low, because known tropes may be considered "safe" for their ability to engage, connect with, and monetize existing relationships with audiences or advertisers. The time has come for journalists and media makers to more aggressively pursue novel approaches to engaging corporeal liberation in narrative, linguistic, or visual and spatial communicative entities. Gaining a firm grip on what is emerging requires a willingness to let go and make a leap into an uncharted future. Concrete recognition of what is to come is always beyond reach, as one must become embedded in the circadian rhythm of each calendar day to be able to make sense of the resulting pace. Reportage like that presented in this chapter is worthwhile because it propels evocative knowing into the forefront of the emotional field.

## Leaning into the Emotional Field

Emotions abound in our age of sharing. Taking my position as a disabled person amid this text, what I am pointing at squarely is the understanding that freedom in American culture has often come with certain accommodations. I use *freedom* with an awareness that it has carried a host of meanings and been abused in the past, so if you prefer I will conceptualize our American freedoms as freedoms along a continuum. Our minds, bodies, spirits, and realities are each encoded with a need for certain accommodations, be they corporeal, geographic, or otherwise. We need in our consideration of who we are, who we wish to become, and how we will work to sustain terra firma, to recognize our freedoms and the continuum along which they exist. Only once we have engaged in that level of authentic disclosure in Christiansian terms can we begin to make sense of the challenging, somewhat uncertain representational work ahead of us. Mediated narration is primed to help us reconceptualize how we see ourselves, opening up a deeper and much needed conversation. We must be open to stepping together into that cultural conversation. In many ways our shared future depends on it.

Even if the activity spans my lifetime and yours, we must allow for generational change to be our barometer of progress, recognizing that the temporal clock of the body is, at least from the perspective of cultural and mediated representation, arguably a timeless pursuit. Let us engage it in such a way that we focus more on the contours of representation than on the length of time necessary to arrive at those more nuanced articulations. We must forgo the pressures of categorization, or at least work actively to ignore them, so that it might be possible to luxuriate in the potentials of a corporeal knowing that may eventually become deeper and more nuanced than we have known throughout the twentieth and twenty-first centuries. More to the point, we must embrace the reality that mediated narration requires a robust recognition of its previous limitations and a firm tug on its doubt-driven roots to conceptualize a body that is both fully articulated and reaching for emancipation.

I admire poet Wendell Berry's candid and pragmatic view about the land as part of us and us as its stewards. As Berry has said: "We don't have a right to ask whether we're going to succeed or not. The only question we have a right to ask is: What's the right thing to do? What does this earth require of us, if we want to continue to live on it?" ("Wendell Berry" 2013, 00:01:07–00:01:22). The crux of Berry's appeal in my view is that he appears, in his writing and public appearances, to love doubt with just the appropriate amount of fervor. Settled in his personal perspective about the importance of sustainable land and living, he nonetheless appears to recognize what is either (1) unknowable to him or (2) unknowable to any human. He is particularly adept at identifying the rhetorics of corporatization, though he would not necessarily characterize himself as performing this activity. Rather, his focus is on gaining enough material, resources, and nourishment so that we all might flourish together. I recognize my own limitations in understanding this work, and any shortcomings in its conceptualization are squarely and entirely my own.

It is in our urban areas, places like the Minneapolis of my upbringing, that we need to redouble our sustainability efforts. The drive to monetize every inch of property, though it will gain cultural approval owing to America's Lockean roots, overlooks a more important conversation about the world as we wish to nurture it: we need to be vulnerable enough to admit that we want a future, even if doing so is not profitable to us today. Author and activist Bill McKibben, who seems closely aligned with Berry's ideas, continually places the environment at the heart of his considerations. What I consider admirable about McKibben's approach, like Berry's, is a principled consistency about the land as a place that we must always return to for our lives and for our living. "He is one of if not the great writer at work in American letters right now . . . And it also happens that it's about the most important subject that we have: whether or not we're going to be able to build the kind of communities that can successfully inhabit this earth or not" said McKibben about Berry ("Wendell Berry" 2013, 00:05:30–00:06:00). I read McKibben's articulations on Berry as containing within them a distinct moral compass anchored in terra firma. Inspired by Berry and McKibben, as a scholar-teacher of journalism I feel called to work toward a more sustainable journalism, which I assert is rooted in Christiansian communitarianism.

Perhaps the most valuable lesson of "Seven Days of Heroin" is this: A body on its own and on its own terms has potential to expand our understanding of the sociocultural challenges of the human condition. We must be willing to lift others when needed. We must not only be good stewards of the land. We must also and especially be good stewards for each other. We must help one another rise, rather than using our power to keep one another from rising. Narrative, longform local reportage, as the case of "Seven Days of Heroin" reveals, has a particularly profound role in that process.

# 5   Storying the Future

I was once told in a blind review of an academic paper that my paper "did not contribute to scholarship in journalism and mass communication." Though I did not keep that review, it is seared into my imagination. I am quite certain that, owing to this critique, I will always be wondering whether and to what extent I truly belong in this academic discipline. Because the review was so scathing, I always work to be charitable in my feedback to students. In every experience, an opportunity. As a scholar-teacher for several years now, I have lived and breathed journalism through the lens of the academy. Inspired by Patricia Hill Collins, I do wonder if writing about journalism as I do represents an "act of resistance" (2015, 107) because I am neither a journalist nor able-bodied and yet I am (also) writing about journalism and able-bodiedness. If it does represent an act of resistance, then let that be as it may. And, if it does not rise to that definition, then I write from the Susan Wendell–inspired standpoint of a disabled person in a disabled body writing about the world at large. I would have never completed this book without the support and encouragement of the students that I have taught and their example of fortitude and determination. During difficult moments across the last several years in my writing process, I imagined myself finishing this book to be a right and proper example to them of persistence (how can I encourage my students to press on if I do not press on myself), and so it would not have made it to publication without their presence. I am grateful to them, forever and always.

I must hope that the lessons I have planned for my students, the scholarship I have authored to date, and the journalism and communication education organizations within which I have conducted service, have qualified me to present a plan regarding a critical poststructuralist future for journalism. I also owe an incredible debt of gratitude in my poststructuralist turn to my mother, whose pragmatism in all she does is continually encouraging me to ask the question "Yes, but why?" This always questioning perspective places me in a beautiful, advantaged, and indeed privileged position as a critical media scholar. I author this book because journalism requires fuller advocacy during a moment when there is much doubt about whether or to what extent journalism should be trusted as a public good in the American cultural imagination. We need journalism more today than at any earlier moment in our country's story.

The most pressing need appears to me to be incisive and dialogic reporting, especially reporting that privileges history and biography, as Christians counsels. The barrage of unfettered content simply underscores the admiration that I feel for working journalists today. My favorite work about this phenomenon remains Kovach and Rosenstiel's *Blur*. Quality is in short supply, and we must protect and defend thorough, fact-based journalism at every available opportunity. I wrote extensively about this need in my first book, *Journalism and Memorialization in the Age of Social Media*. It may well be that the future of the United States depends on the defense of a free and engaged press. I am thinking here not only about the Jeffersonian link between journalism and democracy, but also the historical role of journalism as an arbiter of truth, especially as articulated in Kovach and Rosenstiel's *The Elements of Journalism*. Journalists do not possess objective truth, but they are and, one hopes, always will be striving toward knowledge in a systematic manner, through fact-based writing, reporting, and editing. Journalistic storytelling is vital to making sense of the world. To reiterate Sarah Symonds Leblanc's wise counsel: "By sharing narratives, social constructivists explore and make sense of the world around them" (2016, 111). This overarching process is worthy of celebration and broad scholarly recognition. I am also considering how journalism is entrenched in an American sense of checks and balances. Living in recognition of the experiences I have not had, and admitting the things I do not know, I nonetheless attempt as much as possible in this inquiry to foreground the many things I have been fortunate to experience, study, and work toward understanding. Autoethnographers Carolyn Ellis and Art Bochner have especially taught me to embrace doubt on my scholarly journey, through their personal correspondence with me over the last several years.

I have worked herein to recognize that "doing research focused on human longing, pleasure, pain, loss, grief, suffering, or joy ought to require holding authors to some standard of vulnerability" (Bochner and Ellis 2016, 212). I hope I have succeeded in that regard. I wish the reader to bridge autoethnographic and critical-cultural knowledge bases along with me, in hopes that this bridging might not always seem as novel in the future as it seems to me on this spring morning in 2020. If I am truly fortunate, this book might inspire future books by other writers. In this way I might well be connected to individuals I have not met and may never meet. To return to autoethnographer Cris Davis's dictum: "Stories are a way of knowing and communicating; we connect with each other through our stories" (2008, 415). I do hope others might carry the story of journalism forward, even long after I am gone. I hope I have provided a foundation on which to do some preliminary building. Through the study of the cases in this book, I have tried to do right by the principle that qualitative researchers "study things in their natural settings, attempting to make sense of, or interpret phenomena in terms of the meanings people bring to them" (Denzin and Lincoln 1994, 2). I hope, at least in some small way, to have succeeded insofar as this book is useful and insightful to students and scholars alike.

Yearning for entry into the vast beauty of Wendell Berry's earth, I sometimes ask my partner to drive me to Wrightsville Beach, so that I might bask in the all-encompassing everything of the waves in the Atlantic Ocean. I don't actually ever submerge myself in the water—I prefer to stay seated on the bench on the sand—and I've willed myself to make a promise to go in on my next trip. The realities of the everyday are such that even though I would like to be on that bench every weekend, we make it there about three to four times per year. I bow in gratitude for all I have and for the blessing of the experience. It has become fashionable, as we look toward the next American presidential election in 2020, for all stakeholders across the political spectrum to carry forward conceptualizations of overarching concepts like freedom and security.

We in the United States certainly value both of these principles, but it worries me as a critical-cultural scholar when the concepts are intended to inspire fear or favor on one political side or another. Politicization removes concepts from their home context and places them instead into an all-too-reductive dialogue that merely bolsters one talking point or another for a specific politician during a particular campaign experience. We need in our cultural post-9/11 and post–Sandy Hook moment to do the difficult and prolonged dialogic work of conceptualizing sustainable security. I am admittedly not sure how to do that. But embracing story feels like it might provide a start. Taking an autoethnographic stance, as a person who has never been hunting for food or sport, I struggle to understand the need for high-powered automatic weapons. I also must embrace the vulnerable position that hunting for food or sport is not something that I wish to pursue out of love for all of creation, so I experience difficulty braiding firearms or weapons (automatic or otherwise) of any kind into my narrative experience. Nonetheless I recognize and appreciate that there are those who utilize firearms for food, sport, or personal self-defense. I believe firmly in their right to do that and, following Voltaire, would defend that right. Moreover, individuals who live in the country or in the wilderness, away from urban centers (areas that are sometimes narrated wrongly and derisively as "flyover country") have different needs and wants with firearms. If I lived in a more wooded area, I could imagine purchasing a firearm and learning how to use it for personal protection, in case it became absolutely necessary.

I am, therefore, for all my love of creation in Berryian and McKibbenian senses, nonetheless a rugged individualist of sorts, firmly entrenched in the Lockean ideals of life, liberty, and property that blanket the American experience and perhaps especially the experience of the rural American South in which I currently reside. It is for this reason that, after Sandy Hook, I cannot endorse a "no guns ever" position. But I do think we need sensible, reasonable gun policy in our country. Consenting to live with the continuing trauma of school violence, we risk becoming desensitized to the loss of life. One approach toward a more durable, reasonable, and likely safer approach may be to include firearms training in early educational settings, for the sake of allowing students and teachers alike to make sense of what a firearm is, how it functions, and how it might be deployed if (and only if) necessary. Fear tends to make reasonableness more difficult to approach in American media culture: approaching gun use with a fuller, more deliberate sense of dialogue has considerable potential to be instructive for all. In this section of the book, I am myself trying to do the work I am asking journalists to engage in: difficult questions, contradictions, histories, biographies, lived experiences, and all. It is difficult, to be sure, but I am fortunate for the opportunity. Indeed, I always return to Berry: "The world and our life in it are conditional gifts. We have the world to live in, and the use of it to live from, on the condition that we would take good care of it. To take good care of it, we have to know it and know how to take care of it. And to know it, and to be willing to take care of it, we have to love it" (2013, 10:41–11:20).

I wish to underscore this blessing, to love the earth and do what we can to take care of it, as a basic requirement in free and fair societies, because it is one that is sometimes forgotten amid the drama of our everyday disagreements. To work on engaging in Christiansian communitarianism is an act of love in free and open societies. Our dialogues are important, to be sure, but they are able to rest on a foundation where we rightly exercise our freedoms of thought and movement. For all the conflicted emotions I may experience as a disabled person who is not able to safely drive a car, I know that I am able to move about as I please and can manage on foot, and that I can be driven. One of the blessings of the American cultural landscape is that our freedom and security are fairly well established. Though we may rightly yearn for more freedom and more security, there exists a baseline of these two concepts to which a sizable percentage have access and can enjoy throughout their everyday experiences. I am able to move freely of my own accord, I am even, as I mention above, able to walk when the weather allows it: my range of motion in the world is vast and workable, with accommodations. A blessing.

The poet Basho wrote: "This old village—/ not a single house / without persimmon trees" (in Hass, 53). And so I wonder: what makes any place distinctive? The way forward I might say is to find the hook on which to hang the narrative that guides the story of a particular place. Basho's old village feels familiar, and yet I've never been there. I do know this: along the banks of a river I recognize the power of water guiding so many relations between time, space, and place.

Cartography is valuable because when we assign locations on the map we may also be indicating times and spaces. The cover of my second collection of poetry contains the image of the globe. I have never looked closely at it. In doing so, I recognize that it must be of a different time because I do not recognize the letterings and languages written on it. The vastness of the past is its own welcome invitation, the gift of remembering one's past while also recognizing a land entirely new. The past, present, and future are always in dialogue with one another; how to honor the manifold qualities of each phase certainly represents a life's work. Reflecting on a couple of the childhood stories I have shared, such as those about watching Larkin on television, have reminded me of the depth of geographer Stuart Aitken's perception: "Children see things in environments that we may have forgotten how to see, let alone understand" (2012, 500).

This broad work of meaning-making across epochs will likely inform my future work. I am continually fascinated by isolation and community as rhetorical forces, and I cannot help but wonder whether there are binding agents amid their tensions. Working through those knots evokes for me the process of building, the act of meaningful construction. For now, though, I bow to what is before me, attempting to live in recognition of the truth of what I have just completed. I pause, gaze out the window, orient myself to the dusk outside, and find my bearings. I take stock of what I have built, or, rather, what I have worked to plant in the world. In pondering what it means to be from somewhere, as well as of somewhere. I feel that in calling out these words I am also bowing to a locale on the map, a way of saying thank you.

In shaping a future for journalism, I am leaning most directly on Christians's dictum about authentic disclosure, especially as read through Wendell Berry's conception of stewardship of the earth. I am a scholar who has often found myself around journalism (teaching it, researching it, serving it) in the academy. These experiences have been the foundational elements of my place in the labor force or working world as I have come to live it. I write out of a blend of admiration for the potential of journalistic work and concern about what might be next for journalism in open societies around the world. I ultimately lean toward optimism, but heavy doses of Hall and Poster often encourage me toward a more reasoned pragmatism. The "pain" (Poster 1989, 3) that critical theory seeks to interrogate and ameliorate is real and requires sustained scholarly attention. I am willing and able to endure that pain because I believe, as do Bochner and Ellis, that we autoethnographers " want ourselves and our societies to be better than they are" (2016, 213). But working toward "better" requires sustained labor.

Indeed, we need today not only more and better stories but also more and better journalism education. The communities of journalism practice, of which I am not part, and of journalism pedagogy, of which I am honored to be part, need to seek out opportunities for collaboration and shared resources. My friend, mentor, and colleague Dr. Amy K. Sanders, in the digital initiative *Jumpline Journalism* (https://jumplinejournalism. com/), is part of one such exciting upstart movement connecting journalism educators both to other educators and to practitioners as well. We as teachers need such resources, and our students will certainly benefit from them as well. Recognizing the visual turn in journalism and mass communication, I am also interested in the way still and moving images (especially on social media) engage audiences. In broad terms, I further recognize waning levels of trust in journalism (see, for example, Jahng and Littau [2015, 54]) and am investigating journalism during a period of evolving platforms and professional changes.

Journeys always open as many questions as a scholar can fit between the pages of the bound book. The blessing for professors as authors is the opportunity to focus on their most immediate preoccupations. I am fascinated by the body because I have always had to be extra-mindful and extra-considerate of my own. This act of forced self-care has encouraged me to turn both inward and outward for understanding. In the course of this study I have had the pleasure of being able to turn inward through autoethnography and outward through cultural/critical case study research, in the service of presenting this research about the future of journalism. I appreciate the care with which readers have considered my words. May this book represent a starting point, and may the dialogues continue in the years and decades ahead.

## Conclusion

Complicated issues benefit from a critical poststructuralist approach to journalism. *Mediated Narration in the Digital Age* is a new media technology history that examines mediated narration from 1991 through 2018. I use examples across media culture to call for a communitarian ethos of respect, inclusion, and dialogue in mediated narration. Employing Michel de Certeau in chapter 1, Stuart Hall in chapter 2, Susan Wendell in chapter 3, and Clifford Christians in chapter 4, I use relevant issues, including the mediated body in everyday life and school shootings in times of crisis, to chart a critical poststructuralist future for journalism in our digital age.

I've written this book to bring journalism more closely into alignment with the human experience. I've always found the notion of journalistic objectivity to be flawed and yet have only recently recognized the vocabulary through which to advance this argument. In these pages I hope I have pointed to its flaws in a meaningful way and, importantly, offered a reasonable alternative. I can think of no greater calling than journalism, so my qualms are not with the practice, but rather with the way the practice is all too often carried out. Representations of lived experience on journalistic pages and increasingly on journalistic screens have long appeared much too flat to be believable to me. The human experience is messy and complicated and beautiful, but precious little of that mess and complication and beauty makes it into American and Western journalisms during our present-day sociocultural moment. It is my modest hope that this book begins a movement in earnest to work toward changing that. I specifically hope that journalistic subjectivities are broken open and shared freely, for the false masks of detached observers seem to have little relevance to me to the journalism of the current moment. We need the journalist(s) willing to work to tell the stories of those individuals whose testimonies would otherwise be lost. Reviving journalism in new media culture is an arduous process, but one that has strong potential to prove ultimately worthwhile if this overarching task can be achieved through attention to mediated narration in particular and storying the media world in general.

In this concluding chapter I return with renewed energy to the theoretical underpinnings of the book. Returning to de Certeau's seminal quotation, "Narrated reality constantly tells us what must be believed and what must be done" (186), I see the meaning of his words more deeply. Principally, I recognize the bridge between thought and action. Media influences thought, which may lead to altered, engaged action(s). I distinctly hope journalism adopts a critical poststructuralist approach in order to redouble its attention to pressing issues, including the mediated body in everyday life and school shootings in times of crisis. In the FDR examples and the examples of the heroin epidemic in Ohio and Kentucky, what worries me is that those two issues may fall through the journalistic cracks because they might be overlooked—labeled neither ubiquitous nor timely enough to warrant sustained journalistic attention. We as critical media scholars need to continue investigating how communities are (or are not) represented through mediated reality/ies. A layered narrative of a struggling place might help that place heal over time. Scholarship, like journalism itself, must recognize and embrace its potential value in this broader effort.

Without a doubt, the Christiansian communitarian perspective is at the center of the solution suggested in this book. As Christians writes: "A more sophisticated concept of news, consistent with dialogical ethics, is authentic disclosure. In this perspective, reporting must be grounded historically and biographically, so that complex cultures are represented adequately" (2007, 126). In conducting this study I've come to realize that all five chapters are rooted in "complex cultures." In chapter 1, the mediated body, laden as it is with expectations, arguably presents normative conceptions of what should be aspirational (Mantle's body) and what should be considered of lesser importance, all other body types. Indeed, though I did not include this example in the first chapter, it is worth emphasis here in the conclusion: even a female supermodel's body is arguably at risk, because it is always to be measured against the unachievable ideal of that which the stereotypical white heterosexual male desires—an ever-shifting, often-fickle caricature of a real woman.

In chapter 2, the process of storying Sandy Hook reflects a complex culture because it too easily resolves the seemingly unresolvable: the murder of innocent schoolchildren. As I articulate, seeking journalistic explanation is certainly understandable, but finding it without sufficient investigation is problematic because what result are "operational fictions" (Hall 1974, 23) rather than dialogic understandings.

In chapter 3, the process of storying FDR "being pushed" reflects a complex culture because to be disabled is to be outside the norm of the American and Western media story, and thus the disability is what is too often focused upon. FDR's disabled body is noted for its unusualness because it must "be pushed"—the body itself is unusual because negotiating it becomes a labor not only for FDR but also and especially for someone else, the person doing the pushing. As I underscore, FDR's disabled body requires work, and it is work that the journalist (in only twenty-four seconds) is either unwilling or unable to contribute. What is sacrificed in this coverage, as a result, is an opportunity to have a meaningful dialogue about disability in American and Western culture (see, for example, Wendell [1989]).

In the fourth chapter I present "Seven Days of Heroin" as an exemplar of the Christiansian communitarian ethos. I especially highlight how the reportage explains the complexity of the problem of heroin addiction in Ohio and Kentucky and stories the multiplicity of perspectives (addicts, their families, law enforcement, government officials, health care officials) impacted by that crisis. In that way, this story delves into the complexity of its intersecting cultures in an admirable manner. While there are no easy answers for a community plagued by heroin addiction, shining necessary light on the problem and its myriad elements through long-form narrative storytelling has considerable potential to make significant strides in a promising direction.

As I have worked to articulate across the cases in this book, a critical poststructuralist approach to journalism imbued with a Christiansian communitarian ethos is well equipped to both story communities and inform the public about the issues at the heart of those communities. On the morning of January 26, 2020, I learned of a shooting in the town where I work.

The city issued the following press release:

The Police Department is investigating a shooting that occurred in the early morning hours of January 26th, 2020 in the 100 Block of Camden Avenue. Police were dispatched to the location following a call received at 1:59 a.m. Police say that six people were shot at the scene. Darlington County Coroner Todd Hardee has confirmed that two people were pronounced dead. The others are being treated at local hospitals. SLED and the US Marshal Service are assisting the Police Department in the investigation. The Police Department is currently pursuing leads and anyone with information is asked to call the Investigations Divison [*sic*] at 843.610.0633." ("Police Department Investigating Shooting" 2020)

The quoted section is the entire body of the press release. I do not know any additional information, as of this writing, on that same day. I worry that the press release is too brief, but I know the information is less than twenty-four hours old. This is the reality of the present-day media environment. My heart is worried for my students, colleagues, friends, and fellow citizens. I do not have any additional information about what occurred. My sincere hope is that the reportage in the aftermath of this terrible tragedy might follow a Christiansian communitarian perspective. If it does our community will certainly benefit. This evening the community will hold a prayer vigil, and there are drop-in counseling hours available throughout the week and ostensibly into the foreseeable future. Through the course of these events, I am hopeful conversations will begin and continue toward eventual healing.

Dialogue is a healing tool, used in the right sorts of ways. I believe that Norman K. Denzin and Yvonna S. Lincoln get it correctly: "As a site of discussion or discourse, qualitative research is difficult to define clearly. It has no theory or paradigm that is distinctly its own" (1994, 3). In this study I have taken these words to heart. I view the lack of definition as an opportunity for openness. Robert E. Stake expresses a certain sort of openness in another way: "Perhaps the simplest rule for method in qualitative case work is this: Place the best brains available into the thick of what is going on" (1994, 242). Over the last seven years of working on this book, I have surrounded myself with the best qualitative research—autoethnography, case study, and critical theory—that I could find. Seeking difficult answers has led me to profound insights about commonalities in the qualitative paradigm. All three of these approaches are deeply concerned with power as conveyed through story: (1) who has power, (2) how they obtained that power, and (3) how that power might be reclaimed (and by whom to what ends).

As I have worked to make clear in this book, the cases studied here strongly suggest that power never occurs in a vacuum. Power is better understood as structural exercise: to afford or constrain power is a deliberate practice. As Derrida states, "By orienting and organizing the coherence of the system, the center of the structure permits the play of its elements inside the total form" (1978, 279). The time is ripe for journalists and journalism scholars to consider the structure that undergirds their professional practices. Plainly, journalism conducted without diverse sources cannot serve the interests or needs of diverse populations. The vast majority of cases considered in this book reinforce storytelling themes that build and sustain the powerful. In Derrida's language, the structure of professional media seems largely to support voicing by, of, and for existing stakeholders. What is missing in this configuration, of course, are the voices of those whose interests are not presently being heard, including the groups principally considered in this book, such as the victims of school shootings. I hope that I have emphasized the importance of power as a structural consideration.

To reconfigure voices at the table, or sources employed in a story on a single occasion is not enough. I fear that celebrating outsider voices only or largely as a special event is to marginalize those voices in a sense of what Derrida would consider "play." Representing diverse voices as play compounds their marginalization, because it provides such voices a vantage point in relation to the center without any (or enough) reasonable hope of reaching the center. Indeed, voices all too often excluded from journalistic conversations need to be layered into reportage on a regular basis, until such time as doing so becomes the norm. Braiding Derrida into Hall, the cases in this book strongly suggest that power has only been granted to marginalized or underrepresented groups once their inclusion was accepted as normal. Mediated narration is such important work precisely because to be narrated into the story is one way of being represented, and made visible, within and amid the masses. Derrida seems aware of this reality when he states that "everything begins with structure, configuration or relationship" (1978, 286). Diverse voices need to be *structured* alongside powerful voices as an intentional matter of course correction. To restructure the process of storying the media world is to reimagine it from first principles in a way that opens its norms to needed scrutiny. In our search for diversity, there is a responsibility and an opportunity to recognize, along with qualitative researchers Kara L. Lycke and Ellis Hurd, that "the kinds of personal and social relationships, exchanges, and networks in which we participate are taking new forms" (2017, 292). This newness matters, not only as Silverstone has conceptualized it in new media terms, but also, as Lycke and Hurd note, across "everyday life" (292). An important way to demonstrate that newness matters is to be sure it is represented in mediated narration.

The profession of journalism, and those who study it, must weave newness further into reportage and be willing to be vulnerable about past shortcomings, including missed opportunities to harness the potentially diversifying power of digital and social media. Reorganization through critical theory will no doubt require considerable Posterian "pain" (1989, 3), mostly in the form of admitting past wrongs and charting a more diverse plan ahead. Progress is never easy, though, and the examples studied in this book suggest a path forward is possible. As evidenced by the "Seven Days of Heroin" case, considerable strides have been made. Telling the heroin epidemic through the voices of the affected community/ies normalizes and humanizes that pain. Storying the media world in such a manner does well to make space for challenge a meaningful reality within the human experience. Embracing the complexity of the everyday, as happened in reporting about the heroin epidemic in Ohio and Kentucky, carries with it an opportunity for considerable reorganization of the dominant power structure. But the balance of cases studied in this book suggest that there is much work yet to be done.

As I noted in the introduction, new media technology history has deep, foundational roots. In concluding I wish to discuss those roots a bit further. In "The Computer as a Communication Device" Licklider and Taylor foretold in 1968, "We believe that we are entering a technological age in which we will be able to interact with the richness of living information" (1968, 21). Interaction is certainly taking place in a variety of ways today, but still too much of the interaction is the powerful exchanging information and ideas with the powerful. Braiding Licklider and Taylor into Hall, the choices on the table too often represent a false choice of "This or That" (Hall 1974, 23). For the considerable differences I have already articulated between Mickey Mantle and Gene Larkin, for example, the two baseball players studied in this book also are arguably similar. They are representing their profession as white males who have risen to a level of accomplishment that is only attainable to the elite "best of the best" among their peer group. In Licklider and Taylor's words, the "richness of living information" has barely been accessed when media attention shines brightly on media stars. The choice is barely any choice at all: one (Mantle) the model for the other (Larkin). Licklider and Taylor wrote: "We believe that communicators have to do something nontrivial with the information they send and receive" (1968, 21).

Licklider and Taylor were ostensibly discussing communication as a process, just as I have been discussing storying the media world as a process. To recreate the structure, after all, is to rethink the process by which (or through which) that structure is formed. Studying new media technology history, especially the dynamic twenty-seven—year-period studied here, affords the opportunity to restructure and reprocess mediated narration. After all, not even Licklider and Taylor could have imagined the ease of storying the self into the other in our present-day communication environment. Put simply, the tools to engage a more diverse, pluralistic media audience are at our disposal. It is up to journalists and journalism scholars to make effective use of those tools moving forward. The seven cases presented in this book have, I hope, shed needed light on places where journalism has succeeded and where it has faltered. Taking stock holistically of those successes and failures is, in my view, an opportunity to consider the future of journalism in what Derrida might recognize as its "total form" (1978, 279). In other words, we need to recognize journalism's structuralist past in order to construct its critical, poststructuralist future. Fortunately, we have the shared infrastructure in which to reflect on our past, make progress in the present, and look toward the future: the computer in general and the internet in particular. Licklider and Taylor knew it as "the programmed digital computer," which in 1968 they rightly celebrated as "a common medium that can be contributed to and experimented with by all" (1968, 22). In 2020, now is the time to harness the power of the new medium (new then and still new today, though perhaps in different ways) in a diverse, pluralistic direction. The prescriptions provided across this book (1) presenting nonstar athletes in novel ways, (2) storying the victims of mass shootings more holistically, (3) storying non-able-bodied individuals more deeply into media narratives, and (4) revealing the complexities of pain in the human experience would more fully reflect the "by all" to which Licklider and Taylor were referring more than fifty years ago.

While it will no doubt trouble Derrida's "center," the work of critical poststructuralism must be willing to build that center anew in a more diverse, pluralistic and inclusive manner. And Derrida might even aid in that work, recognizing as he did the presence of the center, any center, in the first place. To theorize about the future of journalism and mass communication is to theorize about a project that allows for participation, especially by those individuals and institutions who have yet to fully participate. Identifying the power relations, the existing structures, their centers and their edges, has been one of the core contributions of this book. In this way, I hope, I have employed not only Derrida but also Licklider and Taylor effectively. The computer is, and long has been, a power structure through which to build a more communitarian shape for the future of journalism and mass communication. Online communities, as I noted in my first book , have sometimes revealed themselves to be decidedly effective entities for "revoicing" (Gloviczki 2015, xiv), well run and equitably organized. The results, in some ways, have afforded those who do not usually have a voice in mass media conversations the opportunity to speak openly, to be and feel heard. The computer has long demonstrated what is possible on a small scale. The future of journalism and mass communication carries the chance to extend that possibility beyond the small scale into larger, more massified audiences.

Admittedly, I am never certain if mass communication as a discipline remains relevant today. I know I am not alone in this concern (see, for example, Chaffee and Metzger [2001]). In my view, masses have become, more appropriately today, fractured or even atomized. But I hold out hope that a more diverse, pluralistic, Christiansian communitarianism may help reorganize, or remassify, the audience. Christiansian communitarian might again inspire the mass to return to mass communication. I recognize that such work may be quite difficult. And I expect that it, too, would be a generations-long effort, like normalizing the disabled body. Simply, I hope the mass might more eagerly gather if they were more fully represented. In this book I have worked to chart a potential path toward fuller representation in and through mediated narration. Progress in that direction will not be without its challenges, but I believe the effort to be worthwhile.

Autoethnographers award the power to the self, by virtue of their presence in human experience, in order to give voice to their lived experiences. Case-study researchers give power to the inductive story contained within "the case itself" (see, for example, Stake [1994]) because there is something novel or remarkable about that case, which can teach researchers how to better model for the future. Critical theorists are concerned with power, especially when it may be a source of "pain" (Poster 1989, 3) and particularly if obtained through structural inequalities, in order to work more fully toward mercy and justice for those not in a position of power. All three approaches are seeking to re-story power and its core dynamics, in the service of eventually producing a more equitable lifeworld within which to participate in the human experience. I am honored to benefit from these research traditions. I hope that I have adequately conveyed my debt to each one. We need all three approaches to story the media world into 2020 and beyond.

In her poem "Parable" Sandra Beasley writes, "Worries come to a man and a woman. / Small ones, light in the hand." (2015, 42). I fear that journalism has, for too long, been preoccupied with presence rather than with representation. This preoccupation likely has stemmed from a genuine desire to be more diverse, perhaps without knowing how to fully engage that desire. Writing this book, and thinking for the last seven years about what it means to story the media world, has helped me become especially attuned to the relationship between language and power (see, for example, Fairclough [2015]). I have already written extensively in this book about common sense and its power, especially regarding Hall's conception of media power. In Faircloughian terms, though, it seems worth emphasizing that "common sense can be a force for certain directions of change or an obstacle to them" (Fairclough 2015, 14). Journalists need to decide what, if anything, will be done with their worries about representation.

Having never actually been a journalist myself, I wonder about the boundaries of my work. Geographer Stuart Aitken has perceptively written, "I wonder at what things should stop my probing, what things I shouldn't write about" (2012, 506). I pause for a moment, only to return to Gerbner and Gross, to the vastness of the communication "environment." This vastness spurs me forward, and I remember how "the environment that sustains the most distinctive aspects of human existence is the environment of symbols" (1976, 173). Though I may not know the journalism world firsthand, I certainly do know the symbolic world firsthand. We all do, each in our own ways. For all my statuses as an outsider, the triangle between case study research and autoethnography and textual analysis is one that I have come to feel as a door inside throughout the seven years of authoring this book. At that intersection of theory-method-praxis I find my way inside.

At the outset I posed two conceptual questions. I return to those questions now in hopes of providing some concrete answers.

1) How are stories being narrated? I use the tools of qualitative research, especially the case study research strategy, autoethnography, and textual analysis to investigate that question. Six of the seven cases studied in this book strongly suggest that mediated narration reinforces the positions of those already in power. To tell a story about the powerful in a way that keeps them in power is the most easily visualizable way to engage in mediated narration. The powerful are "camera ready" and known to the audience; their roles are easily quantifiable in tight, deadline narratives. Mantle is undeniably the star. Larkin, as the pinch hitter, stands in as such, too. While engaging in mediated narration in this

manner is certainly problematic, as I have articulated throughout the book, it is also a systematic pattern, one which will take a considerable amount of intentionality to upend. As the one outlier to the norm, the case of "Seven Days of Heroin" strongly suggests that it might be possible, with generations-long effort, to build the system anew. I am, therefore, optimistic for a future in mediated narration that is more diverse and pluralistic than it has been in the past.

2) What might be the impact on the audience of narrating stories in that way? I am employing a critical, poststructuralist theoretical lens to investigate that question. Six of the seven cases studied in this book portray audiences as mostly white, athletic, already powerful, upper class, able-bodied, and usually male. An audience outside of any of these categories seems unlikely to see, hear, or feel themselves represented in mediated narration. The one case that did offer audiences a more diverse portrayal, "Seven Days of Heroin," has the potential to reorganize the audience around a more human and humane consideration of the realities of the lived experience. Principally, the nuanced portrayals of the challenges associated with the heroin epidemic in Ohio and Kentucky suggest that media entities are potentially well positioned to help audiences work through community challenges and problems together. In pragmatic terms, media coverage of this type serves to raise awareness about the ways that crisis impact tends to be broad and deep across affected societies.

I consider it a privilege to have had the opportunity to use these three research methodologies (the case study research strategy, autoethnography, and textual analysis), to use critical theory, and to use my vantage point as a person with a physical disability, to undertake this study. I recognize that others who engaged in this same work may reach slightly different conclusions than I did. However, I expect that if others did the same work, they would also be quite unlikely to see themselves or many people like themselves in mediated narration throughout the period studied here. I am fairly confident that the findings presented here are both valid and replicable. Humans are far more diverse than even the most forgiving of categories enforced in most instances of mediated narration. Mediated narration unfortunately still has a long way to go to represent us. The process of engaging in this research has considerably raised my awareness about that reality.

For that truth, I am deeply grateful. I hope and expect that perhaps you, too, dear reader, have been impacted in a similar way. I invite other researchers to begin storying cases, autoethnographic experiences, and textual analyses into the media world. Continued research in this arena may open new paths for visibility and representation. Christians's call for more diverse, representation rings as urgently as ever today. In our increasingly atomized media environment, the enduring impact of narrating stories in a more pluralistic way might be to regain a robust sense of the "mass" in mass communication. As I have gestured toward often, Licklider and Taylor in 1968 recognized the possibilities for fuller representation through technology. The cases I have studied herein strongly suggest that mediated narration is not there yet. I do await the moment, with some optimism, when those representational possibilities will be achieved, in and for new media technology history.

The power of mediated narration has the potential to drive or stifle the next generation of mediated representation. The cases studied in this book point out some reasons for optimism and also raise some cause for concern. Optimism is centered in "Seven Days of Heroin," and concern arises from the untapped potential of the digital and social media infrastructure. The work of each will require considerable struggle, a struggle that will either be focused on building something new or on maintaining the existing practices. The cases considered here suggest that the future is unlikely to arrive as an all-or-nothing proposition. In the twenty-seven years studied here, one of seven cases reflects diverse, pluralistic representation. My modest hope is that when similar studies are conducted thirty to fifty years from now, the number of cases in the affirmative might rise to three or four out of seven. Change is certainly a slow process, but incremental evidence of progress is and must be recognized as valuable. Concluding this book, I am cautiously optimistic that the future of mediated narration will gradually reveal more successes than failures.

Connections appear where doors are open. How fortunate those of us who do qualitative research are for the doors that it continues to open for us. Journalism and mass communication, as they look to story the media world into the next decade, have a particular opportunity to tell challenging stories in new and novel ways. May the practitioners, scholars, and educators in this community, as they engage in dialogue, remember

Wendell Berry's words: "We don't have a right to ask whether we're going to succeed or not. The only question we have a right to ask is: What's the right thing to do? What does this earth require of us, if we want to continue to live on it?" ("Wendell Berry" 2013, 00:01:07–00:01:22). With a Christiansian communitarian perspective there does seem to be hope for a Berryian "right thing": a more pluralistic, diverse, humane, and, I hope, sustainable future for journalism and mass communication.

# Source Acknowledgments

An earlier version of chapter 1 (with a different title) was presented at the 2016 North American Society for the Sociology of Sport (NASSS) conference in Tampa, Florida. I am grateful to Lawrence Wenner for chairing the panel on media stars in which it was included, and to the other panelists in that session and the audience members for their support of and feedback about the work. Another part of chapter 1 (in an earlier version and with a different title) was presented at the 2016 Carolinas Communication Association (CCA) conference in Wilmington, North Carolina. I am grateful to the members of the panel within which it was presented as well as to audience members at the conference for their thoughtful insights.

I am grateful to the entire staff at the Vanderbilt Television News Archive, where I spent a wonderful week researching in July 2015. It was on that research trip that I gained access to the Mantle coverage cited in this book, as well as much of the other television news coverage cited throughout.

Special thanks to the producers and distributors of *Soccer Shrines* for their willingness to provide me with free electronic access to the "Glasgow" episode that is cited in this book.

I am grateful to Carolyn Ellis and Art Bochner for feedback on an early draft of this book. Their insightful comments helped me recognize that media narratives, especially media power (as conceptualized by Stuart Hall), are vital to this book.

A portion of chapter 3 began (with a different title) as a conference paper at the 2017 International Congress for Qualitative Inquiry. I am grateful to the panelists in the memory panel that I participated in for their support and feedback.

Large portions of my autoethnographic vignette in chapter 4 have been used as my teaching and diversity statements, respectively. They are previously unpublished. I include them here because they speak to my understanding of community.

Portions of chapter 5 began as a coauthored paper with Kasi Williamson that was submitted to and rejected by *The Qualitative Report* (*TQR*). I thank the editor of *TQR* as well as an anonymous reviewer for their feedback. I kept the best parts of my writing in that paper and restructured or discarded the rest. I am the sole author of chapter 5. The feedback received in all instances helped reveal connections between them that eventually led to this book. Without Williamson's patience in responding to my emails, I am quite certain this book would have never been completed. I owe her a debt of gratitude for being so patient with me.

# References

"1991 WS Gm7: Larkin's Single Wins Series for Twins." 2013. MLB YouTube Channel. October 13, 2013. www.youtube.com/watch?v=QYuWVArJbBM.

Aitken, Stuart C. 2012. "Young Men's Violence and Spaces of Addiction: Opening up the Locker Room." *Social & Cultural Geography* 13 (2): 127–43. doi: 10.1080/14649365.2012.655767.

Alcoff, Linda. 1988. "Cultural Feminism versus Post-Structuralism: The Identity Crisis in Feminist Theory." *Signs: Journal of Women in Culture and Society* 13 (3): 405–36. doi: 10.1086/494426.

Alley, Robert S. 1985. "Values on View: A Moral Myopia?" *Critical Studies in Mass Communication* 2 (4): 395–406. doi: 10.1080/15295038509360102.

Beasley, Sandra. 2015. *Count the Waves: Poems.* New York: Norton.

Berger, Peter L., and Thomas Luckmann. 1967. *The Social Construction of Reality: A Treatise in the Sociology of Knowledge.* New York: Penguin.

Berry, Keith. 2006. "Implicated Audience Member Seeks Understanding: Reexamining the 'Gift' of Autoethnography." *International Journal of Qualitative Methods* 5 (3): 94–108. doi: 10.1177/160940690600500309.

Blumler, Jay G., and Elihu Katz.1974. *The Uses of Mass Communications: Current Perspectives on Gratifications Research.* Thousand Oaks CA: Sage.

Bochner, Arthur P. 2006. "Janice's Voice." *Southern Communication Journal* 71 (2): 183–93. doi: 10.1080/10417940600683554.

———. 2012. "On First-Person Narrative Scholarship." *Narrative Inquiry* 22 (1): 155–64. doi: 10.1075/ni.22.1.10boc.

Bochner, Arthur P., and Carolyn Ellis. 2016. "The ICQI and the Rise of Autoethnography: Solidarity through Community." *International Review of Qualitative Research* 9 (2): 208–17. doi: 10.1525/irqr.2016.9.2.208.

Bodenhamer, David J. 2015. "Narrating Space and Place." In *Deep Maps and Spatial Narratives*, edited by David J. Bodenhamer, John Corrigan, and Trevor M. Harris, 17–27. Bloomington: Indiana University Press.

Bodenhamer, David J., John Corrigan, and Trevor M. Harris, editors. 2015. *Deep Maps and Spatial Narratives.* Bloomington: Indiana University Press.

Bogle, John C. 2017. *The Little Book of Common Sense Investing: The Only Way to Guarantee Your Fair Share of Stock Market Returns*. Hoboken NJ: Wiley.

boyd, danah. 1995. "'In or Out' by Ani DiFranco." *In or Out*, Www.Danah.Org /Ani/Imperfectly/Inorout.Html.

———. 2015. *It's Complicated: The Social Lives of Networked Teens*. New Haven CT: Yale University Press.

Boylorn, Robin M. 2008. "As Seen on TV: An Autoethnographic Reflection on Race and Reality Television." *Critical Studies in Media Communication* 25 (4): 413–33. doi: 10.1080/15295030802327758.

———. 2013. "'Sit with Your Legs Closed!' and Other Sayin's from My Childhood." *The Handbook of Autoethnography*, edited by S. Holman Jones. Walnut Creek CA: Left Coast, 173–85.

Brison, Susan J. 2008. "Everyday Atrocities and Ordinary Miracles, or Why I (Still) Bear Witness to Sexual Violence (But Not Too Often)." *WSQ: Women's Studies Quarterly* 36 (1–2): 188–98. doi: 10.1353/wsq.0.0060.

Butterworth, Michael L. 2007. "Race in 'The Race': Mark McGwire, Sammy Sosa, and Heroic Constructions of Whiteness." *Critical Studies in Media Communication* 24 (3): 228–44. doi: 10.1080/07393180701520926.

Camus, Albert. 2018. *The Myth of Sisyphus*. Translated by Justin O'Brien. New York: Vintage.

Carey, James W. 2009. *Communication as Culture: Essays on Media and Society*. New York: Routledge.

Chaffee, Steven H., and Miriam J. Metzger. 2001. "The End of Mass Communication?" *Mass Communication and Society* 4 (4): 365–79. doi: 10.1207/s15327825mcs0404_3.

Chancellor, John. 1968. *Urban Affairs / Studies*. Vanderbilt Television News Archive. December 11, 1968. tvnews.vanderbilt.edu/broadcasts/441042.

Christians, Clifford G. 2007. "Utilitarianism in Media Ethics and Its Discontents." *Journal of Mass Media Ethics* 22 (2–3): 113–31. doi: 10.1080/08900520701315640.

Cincinnati.com. 2017. "Seven Days of Heroin: This Is What an Epidemic Looks Like." USA Today Facebook page. Accessed November 16, 2020. www.facebook.com/usatoday/videos/10157512094629698/?notif_id= 1593438420667523¬if_t=mention.

*Cincinnati Enquirer*. 2017. "Seven Days of Heroin: This Is What an Epidemic Looks Like." September 10, 2017. Accessed November 16, 2020. www .cincinnati.com/pages/interactives/seven-days-of-heroin-epidemic -cincinnati/.

Collins, Patricia Hill. 2015. *Black Feminist Thought: Knowledge, Consciousness, and the Politics of Empowerment*. New York: Routledge.

Considine, Bob. 1999. "Louis Knocks Out Schmeling." In *The Best American Sports Writing of the Century*, edited by David Halberstam, 138–39. New York: Houghton Mifflin.

Coonfield, Gordon, and John Huxford. 2009. "News Images as Lived Images: Media Ritual, Cultural Performance, and Public Trauma." *Critical Studies in Media Communication* 26 (5): 457–79. doi: 10.1080/15295030903325354.

Costello, Tom. 2007. *Virginia Tech / Massacre / The Internet*. Vanderbilt Television News Archive. April 17, 2007. tvnews.vanderbilt.edu/broadcasts /865000?.

Crick, Nathan. 2009. "The Search for a Purveyor of News: The Dewey/ Lippmann Debate in an Internet Age." *Critical Studies in Media Communication* 26 (5): 480–97. doi: 10.1080/15295030903325321.

Davies, B., and S. Gannon. 2011. "Feminist/Poststructuralism." *Theory and Methods in Social Research*, edited by B. Somekh and C. Lewin, 2nd ed., 312–19. Thousand Oaks C A: Sage.

Davis, Christine S. 2008. "A Funeral Liturgy: Death Rituals as Symbolic Communication." *Journal of Loss and Trauma*, 13 (5): 406–21. doi: 10.1080/15325020802171391.

Davis, Lennard J. 2016. *The Disability Studies Reader*. 5th ed. New York: Routledge.

de Certeau, Michel. 1988. *The Practice of Everyday Life*. Translated by Steven Rendell. Berkeley: University of California Press.

DeFoster, Ruth. 2017. *Terrorizing the Masses: Identity, Mass Shootings, and the Media Construction of Terror*. New York: Peter Lang.

Denzin, Norman K. 1989. *Interpretive Interactionism*. Thousand Oaks C A: Sage.

———. 1996. "More Rare Air: Michael Jordan on Michael Jordan." *Sociology of Sport Journal*, 13 (4): 319–24. doi: 10.1123/ssj.13.4.319.

———. 2011. *Department of Anthropology: Writing Across Boundaries*. Durham University. Accessed October 28, 2020. www.dur.ac.uk /writingacrossboundaries/writingonwriting/normandenzin/.

Denzin, Norman K., and Yvonna S. Lincoln, editors. 1994. Preface. In *Handbook of Qualitative Research*, ix–xii. Thousand Oaks: Sage.

Derrida, Jacques. 1978. *Writing and Difference*. Translated by Alan Bass. Chicago: University of Chicago Press.

de Zengotita, Thomas. 2005. *Mediated: How the Media Shapes Your World and the Way You Live in It*. New York: Bloomsbury.

*Draft Day*. 2014. "Why Did You Hate Your Father?" (scene 5/10). Accessed November 20, 2020. Movieclips YouTube Channel, February 28, 2017. www .youtube.com/watch?v=lnfpTgAQ0Ys.

Eighmey, John, and Lola McCord. 1998. "Adding Value in the Information Age: Uses and Gratifications of Sites on the World Wide Web." *Journal of Business Research*. www.sciencedirect.com/science/article/abs/pii /S0148296397000611.

Ellis, Carolyn. 1999. "Heartful Autoethnography." *Qualitative Health Research* 9, no. 5: 669–83. doi: 10.1177/104973299129122153.

———. 2003. "Grave Tending: With Mom at the Cemetery." *Forum Qualitative Sozialforschung / Forum: Qualitative Social Research*. https://www.qualitative -research.net/index.php/fqs/article/view/701/1520.

———. 2004. *The Ethnographic I: A Methodological Novel about Autoethnography*. Walnut Creek CA: AltaMira.

Ellis, Carolyn, Tony E. Adams, and Arthur P. Bochner. 2011. "Autoethnography: An Overview." *Forum Qualitative Sozialforschung / Forum: Qualitative Social Research*. www.qualitative-research.net/index.php/fqs/article/view/1589 /3095.

"Faces In The Crowd—Peter's Not Your Average 9-Year-Old." 1993. *Post Bulletin*. Accessed October 28, 2020. www.postbulletin.com/faces-in-the -crowd-peter-s-not/article_81db6f45-af9a-572c-abad-cda75114b02e.html.

Fairclough, Norman. 2015. *Language and Power*. 3rd. ed. New York: Routledge.

"FDR Footage Shows President in Wheelchair." 2013. CBS News YouTube Channel. Accessed October 28, 2020. https://www.youtube.com/watch?v= mzDAWb0XrrE.

*Fink, Conrad. 2003. Writing to Inform and Engage: The Essential Guide to Beginning News and Magazine Writing. In* "Episode 76: A Very Very Very Useful Word." *Grammar Grater*. Luke Taylor. 2008. Accessed October 28, 2020. https://minnesota.publicradio.org/radio/podcasts/grammar_grater /archive/2008/12/11/.

Florini, Sarah. 2014. "Recontextualizing the Racial Present: Intertextuality and the Politics of Online Remembering." *Critical Studies in Media Communication* 31 (4): 314–26. doi: 10.1080/15295036.2013.878028.

Foucault, Michel. 1978. *The History of Sexuality: An Introduction*. New York: Pantheon.

Fox, Ragan. 2014. "Are Those Germs in Your Pocket, or Am I Just Crazy to See You? An Autoethnographic Consideration of Obsessive-Compulsive Disorder." *Qualitative Inquiry* 20 (8): 966–75. doi: 10.1177/1077800413513732.

Gandy, Oscar H. 1982. *Beyond Agenda Setting: Information Subsidies and Public Policy*. Norwood NJ: Ablex.

Gans, Herbert J. 2004. *Deciding What's News: A Study of CBS Evening News, NBC Nightly News, Newsweek, and Time.* Evanston IL: Northwestern University Press.

Gerbner, George, and Larry Gross. 1976. "Living with Television: The Violence Profile." *Journal of Communication* 26 (2): 172–99. https://doi.org/10.1111/j .1460-2466.1976.tb01397.x.

Gingrich-Philbrook, Craig. 2013. "A Knock at the Door." *Departures in Critical Qualitative Research* 3 (1): 24–36. doi:10.1525/dcqr.2014.3.1.24.

Gloviczki, Peter Joseph. 2020. "Always a Student of Autoethnography." *NSUWorks.* nsuworks.nova.edu/tqr/vol25/iss1/13/.

———. 2015. *Journalism and Memorialization in the Age of Social Media.* New York: Palgrave Macmillan.

———. 2016. "Leaving London: Three Autoethnographic Sketches." *Journal of Loss and Trauma* 21 (4): 286–89. doi:10.1080/15325024.2015.1067093.

Goodhead, Andrew. 2010. "A Textual Analysis of Memorials Written by Bereaved Individuals and Families in a Hospice Context." *Mortality* 15 (4): 323–39. doi: 10.1080/13576275.2010.513164.

Griffin, Em. 2003. *A First Look at Communication Theory.* New York: McGraw-Hill Higher Education.

Gurak, Laura J. 2003. *Cyberliteracy: Navigating the Internet with Awareness.* New Haven CT: Yale University Press.

Hall, Stuart. 1974. "Media Power: The Double Bind." *Journal of Communication* 24 (4): 19–26. doi: 10.1111/j.1460-2466.1974.tb00404.x.

———. 1995. "The Whites of Their Eyes: Racist Ideologies and the Media." In *Gender, Race, and Class in Media: A Critical Reader,* edited by Gail Dines and Jean Humez, 18–22. Thousand Oaks CA: Sage.

Hanson, Ralph E. 2018. *Mass Communication: Living in a Media World.* 7th ed. Thousand Oaks CA: Sage.

Hardt, Hanno. 1988. "Comparative Media Research: The World According to America." *Critical Studies in Mass Communication* 5 (2): 129–46. doi: 10.1080/15295038809366693.

Hass, Robert, editor. 1995. *The Essential Haiku: Versions of Basho, Buson, and Issa (The Essential Poets).* New York: Ecco.

Hermida, Alfred. 2016. *Tell Everyone: Why We Share & Why It Matters.* Toronto: Anchor Canada.

Hess, Aaron. 2009. "Resistance Up in Smoke: Analyzing the Limitations of Deliberation on YouTube." *Critical Studies in Media Communication* 26 (5): 411–34. doi: 10.1080/15295030903325347.

"How Many School Shootings Have There Been in 2018 So Far?" 2018. *Guardian*, Guardian News and Media. May 18, 2018. www.theguardian.com /world/2018/feb/14/school-shootings-in-america-2018-how-many-so-far.

The Howard County Poetry and Literature Society. 2012. "Carolyn Forché talks about the poetry of witness." The Howard County Poetry and Literature Society YouTube Channel. March 9, 2012. Date of Access October 28, 2020. https://www.youtube.com/watch?v=TsbMHshfla8.

Huckaby, M. Francyne. 2017. "Becoming Cyborg." *International Review of Qualitative Research* 10 (4): 340–59. doi: 10.1525/irqr.2017.10.4.340.

Jago, Barbara J. 1996. "Postcards, Ghosts, and Fathers: Revising Family Stories." *Qualitative Inquiry* 2 (4): 495–516.

———. 2004. "The Car Radio: An Autoethnographic Short Story." *Journal of Loss and Trauma* 10 (1): 1–6. doi: 10.1080/15325020490890598.

Jahng, Mi Rosie, and Jeremy Littau. 2015. "Interacting Is Believing." *Journalism & Mass Communication Quarterly* 93 (1): 38–58. doi: 10.1177/1077699015606680.

Johnson, Amber Lauren. 2014. "Confessions of a Video Vixen: My Autocritography of Sexuality, Desire, and Memory." *Text and Performance Quarterly* 34 (2): 182–200. doi: 10.1080/10462937.2013.879991.

———. 2017. "From Academe, to the Theatre, to the Streets: My Autocritography of Aesthetic Cleansing and Canonical Exception in the Wake of Ferguson." *Qualitative Inquiry* 24 (2): 88–100. doi: 10.1177/1077800416684869.

Jones, Stacy Holman. 2013. "An Opening to Dream." *Departures in Critical Qualitative Research* 3 (1): 1–5. doi: 10.1525/dcqr.2014.3.1.1.

Katz, Elihu, Jay G. Blumler, and Michael Gurevitch. 1973. "Uses and Gratifications Research." *Public Opinion Quarterly* 37 (4): 509–23. https://doi .org/10.1086/268109.

Kivisto, Peter. 2017. *The Anthem Companion to Robert Park*. London: Anthem.

Leblanc, Sarah Symonds. 2016. "Goodbye, Daddy: An Autoethnographic Journey through the Grief and Mourning Process." *Journal of Loss and Trauma* 22 (2): 110–19. doi: 10.1080/15325024.2016.1192450.

Licklider, J. C. R., and R. Taylor. 1968. "The Computer As a Communication Device." 1990. Reprinted from *Science and Technology*, April 1968. web.stanford .edu/dept/SUL/library/extra4/sloan/mousesite/Secondary/Licklider.pdf.

Lindgren, Simon, and Maxime Lélièvre. 2009. "In the Laboratory of Masculinity: Renegotiating Gender Subjectivities in MTV's Jackass." *Critical Studies in Media Communication* 26 (5): 393–410. doi: 10.1080/15295030903325313.

*Los Angeles Times*. 2014. "7.9 Alaska Earthquake: No tsunami threat for Pacific Coast." June 23, 2014. Accessed December 17, 2014. http://www.latimes.com/local/lanow/la-me-ln-8-0-alaska-earthquake-no -tsunami-threat-forpacific-coast-20140623-story.html.

Lycke, K. L., and E. Hurd. 2017. "Questions of Changing Access: Who Participates in School Ethnographies and Why?" *International Review of Qualitative Research* 10 (3): 291–305. doi: 10.1525/irqr.2017.10.3.291.

Manning, J., and T. E. Adams. 2015. "Popular Culture Studies and Autoethnography: An Essay on Method." *The Popular Culture Studies Journal* 3 (1–2): 187–222.

Marwick, Alice, and Nicole B. Ellison. 2012. "'There Isn't Wifi in Heaven!' Negotiating Visibility on Facebook Memorial Pages." *Journal of Broadcasting & Electronic Media*, 56 (3): 378–400. doi: 10.1080/08838151.2012.705197.

McKee, Alan. 2003. *Textual Analysis: A Beginner's Guide*. Thousand Oaks CA: Sage.

McLuhan, Marshall. 1994. *Understanding Media: The Extensions of Man*. Cambridge MA: MIT Press.

Méndez, Mariza G. 2014. "Autoethnography as a Research Method: Advantages, Limitations and Criticisms." *Colombian Applied Linguistics Journal* 15 (2): 279–87. doi: 10.14483/udistrital.jour.calj.2013.2.a09.

Merwin, William Stanley. 2005. *Migration: New & Selected Poems*. Port Townsend WA: Copper Canyon.

"The Myth of Roosevelt's Wheelchair." 2013. *Time* YouTube Channel. July 17, 2013. Accessed October 28, 2020. www.youtube.com/watch?v=NMKCOb03S-k.

"Newtown Massacre: A Timeline of Events." 2012. CBS News YouTube Channel. December 17, 2012. Accessed on October 28, 2020. www.youtube .com/watch?v=Y7uv3zqSq9o.

"Operation Bullpen." 2003. FBI. October 15, 2003. archives.fbi.gov/archives /news/stories/2003/october/bullpen_101503.

Ott, Brian L., and Robert L. Mack. 2013. *Critical Media Studies: An Introduction*. Malden MA: Wiley.

Ott, Brian, and Cameron Walter. 2000. "Intertextuality: Interpretive Practice and Textual Strategy." *Critical Studies in Media Communication* 17 (4): 429– 46. doi: 10.1080/15295030009388412.

Pate, Joshua R. 2011. "Aigne." *Aigne 2011: Defining Disability*. publish.ucc.ie /aigne/2011/01/pate/02/en.

"Police Department Investigating Shooting." January 26, 2020. Press release emailed to author.

Poster, Mark. 1989. *Critical Theory and Poststructuralism: In Search of a Context*. Ithaca NY: Cornell University Press.

Postman, Neil. 1985. *Amusing Ourselves to Death: Public Discourse in the Age of Show Business*. New York: Viking.

Quan-Haase, Anabel. 2008. "Instant Messaging on Campus: Use and Integration in University Students' Everyday Communication." *The Information Society*, 24 (2): 105–15. doi: 10.1080/01972240701883955.

Rambo, Carol. 2005. "Impressions of Grandmother." *Journal of Contemporary Ethnography* 34 (5): 560–85. doi: 10.1177/0891241605279079.

———. 2007. "Sketching as Autoethnographic Practice." *Symbolic Interaction* 30 (4): 531–42. doi: 10.1525/si.2007.30.4.531.

Rather, Dan, and Vicki Mabry. 1995. "Vanderbilt Television News Archive." *Mantle Funeral | Vanderbilt Television News Archive*. tvnews.vanderbilt.edu /broadcasts/364798.

Reed-Danahay, Deborah. 2017. "Autoethnography." *Oxford Bibliographies Online Datasets*. doi: 10.1093/obo/9780199766567–0162.

Rich, Adrienne. 2013. *The Dream of a Common Language: Poems 1974–1977*. New York: Norton.

Richards, Rose. 2013. "Writing the Othered Self: Autoethnography and the Problem of Objectification in Writing about Illness and Disability." In *Autoethnography*, edited by Pat Sikes, vol. 4, 83–101. Thousand Oaks CA: Sage.

Richardson, Laurel. 1991. "Postmodern Social Theory: Representational Practices." *Sociological Theory* 9 (2): 173–79.

———. 2007. *Last Writes: A Daybook for a Dying Friend (Writing Lives)*. Walnut Creek CA: Left Coast.

Rojas, Rick, and Kristin Hussey. 2017. "Newtown Is 'Still So Raw' 5 Years after Sandy Hook Shooting." *New York Times*. December 13, 2017. www.nytimes .com/2017/12/13/nyregion/newtown-sandy-hook-five-year-anniversary.html.

"Seven Days of Heroin: This Is What an Epidemic Looks Like." *Seven Days of Heroin*. USA Today Facebook Page. www.facebook.com/usatoday/videos /10157512094629698/?notif_id=1593438420667523¬if_t=mention.

Shannon, Claude, and Warren Weaver. 1964. *The Mathematical Theory of Communication*. Urbana: University of Illinois Press.

Shumate, David. 2008. *The Floating Bridge: Prose Poems*. Pittsburgh: University of Pittsburgh Press.

Sikes, Pat. 2013. *Autoethnography*. 4 vols. Thousand Oaks CA: Sage.

Silverstone, Roger. 1999. "What's New about New Media?" *New Media & Society* 1 (1): 10–12. doi: 10.1177/1461444899001001002.

Soccer Shrines. 2018. Password-protected website accessed on February 14, 2018, by permission of the producers of Soccer Shrines. https://www.vimeo .com/255794434.

"Soccer Shrines Glasgow." 2010. Soccer Shrines Glasgow. TVS Vimeo Channel. Accessed February 14, 2018. vimeo.com/255794434.

Sproule, J. Michael. 1989. "Progressive Propaganda Critics and the Magic Bullet Myth." *Critical Studies in Mass Communication* 6 (3): 225–46. doi: 10.1080/15295038909366750.

Stahl, Roger. 2006. "Have You Played the War on Terror?" *Critical Studies in Media Communication* 23 (2): 112–30. doi: 10.1080/07393180600714489.

Stake, Robert E. 1994. "Case Studies." In *Handbook of Qualitative Research*, edited by Norman K. Denzin and Yvonna S. Lincoln, 236–47. Thousand Oaks CA: Sage.

Taylor, Luke. 2008. "Episode 76: A Very Useful Word" *Grammar Grater*. Accessed October 28, 2020. https://minnesota.publicradio.org/radio/podcasts/grammar_grater/archive/2008/12/11/.

Ulmer, Jasmine B. 2017. "Food, Water, Shelter, Justice, Love." *International Review of Qualitative Research* 10 (4): 378–94. doi: 10.1525/irqr.2017.10.4.378.

Uotinen, Johanna. 2014. "Autoethnography in Media Studies: Digitalization of Television in Finland, or Carrying Home Cardboard Boxes." In *The International Encyclopedia of Media Studies*, edited by Fabienne Darling-Wolf, 217–35. New York: Wiley.

Wall, Sarah. 2008. "Easier Said than Done: Writing an Autoethnography." *International Journal of Qualitative Methods* 7 (1): 38–53. doi: 10.1177/160940690800700103.

"Wendell Berry: Poet and Prophet." 2013. PBS. October 3, 2013. www.pbs.org/video/moyers-company-wendell-berry-poet-and-prophet/.

Wendell, Susan. 1989. "Toward a Feminist Theory of Disability." *Hypatia* 4 (2): 104–24. doi: 10.1111/j.1527-2001.1989.tb00576.x.

Wilson, Amy. 2018. "Enquirer Wins Pulitzer Prize for Seven Days of Heroin Coverage." *Cincinnati Enquirer*, April 16, 2018. https://www.cincinnati.com/story/news/2018/04/16/enquirer-wins-pulitzer-prize-seven-days-heroin-coverage/521772002/.

Wong, Sophia Isako. 2002. "At Home with Down Syndrome and Gender." *Hypatia* 17 (3): 89–117. doi: 10.1353/hyp.2002.0071.

Wyatt, Jonathan. 2013. "Always in Thresholds." *Departures in Critical Qualitative Research* 3 (1): 8–17. doi: 10.1525/dcqr.2014.3.1.8.

Yagoda, Ben. 1998. Preface. In *The Art of Fact: A Historical Anthology of Literary Journalism*, edited by Kevin Kerrane and Ben Yagoda, 13–16. New York: Simon and Schuster.

# Index

Abbott, Jim, 14

*ABC News*, 72

the able-bodied, 38, 66, 102

action(s): celebration as, 26; and journalism, 34; mediated narration prescribing, 8, 21, 40; the present in, 82; reflection as, 33; remembrance as, 28; and thought, 114. *See also* faith to action

acts of resistance, 38, 39, 107

Adams, Tony E., 3, 5, 11, 90

addicts and addiction, 25, 93, 102, 116

Aitken, Stuart, 92, 100–101, 112, 122

Ali (fictional character), 24–25

Alley, Robert S., 7

American culture, 56, 59, 79, 91, 95, 103, 115

*An American Family* (PBS), 86

Aristotle, 85

athletes, 26, 27, 28, 37, 38, 120

audiences: acceptance of reductivism by, 6; action, absolved from, 30, 32; action, called to, 33–35, 96, 98–99, 100, 103; adoration of bodies by, 20; of aspirational narrative, 27–28; and journalists, 70, 71, 92; media influencing, 5, 17; of mediated narration, 2, 16–17, 21, 40, 50, 84, 122–23; and narratives of bodies, 47, 77; and news sources, 53, 55–

56; as part of sports team, 28–29; and public representations, 3; and shooting victims, 58, 59; and sports reporters, 18, 26, 27, 98; and technology, 102

autoethnography, 11, 62–64, 88; examples of, 64–65, 89–91; media, 63; as methodology, 43, 62, 87, 122; and power, 117, 121; uses of, 1, 2–3, 5, 12–13, 44, 113

banner graphic of CBS, 67–70

Basho (poet), 111

Beasley, Sandra, 121

Berger, Arthur Asa, 88

Berger, Peter L., 17

Berry, Keith, 15

Berry, Wendell, 9, 104–5, 110–11, 112, 124–25

*The Best Sportswriting of the Century* (Halberstam), 18

Blumler, Jay G., 4, 85

Bochner, Arthur B., 3, 5, 11, 13, 81, 88, 96, 108, 112

Bodenhamer, David J., 46

body(ies): and external conditions, 20, 46–47, 48; of heroes, 26, 27; and heroin use, 35; journeys of, 39; on the line, 47–48; narration of, 47, 76–77, 83–84; as own constraint,

fear, 102, 110

fictions, operational, 8, 50–51, 53–56, 60, 61, 101, 115

*A First Look at Communication Theory* (Griffin), 41–42

Florini, Sarah, 8

Foucault, Michel, 87

Franklin College, 31, 73

Franklin Delano Roosevelt Found Footage: case narrative of, appearance, 67–68; case narrative of, subject of, 70–73; case narrative of, time passage explained, 68–69; case narrative of, wrap-up, 73–75; disabled hero evident in, 79; lessons from, 30–32; methodology used with, 66; overview of, 23; shortcomings in, 9; theory applied to, 65–66; video-sharing of, 36–37. *See also* FDR (Franklin Delano Roosevelt)

freedom(s), 49, 59, 77, 78, 102, 103–4, 109, 111

friend, as theme, 9, 94, 95, 96, 97

Gannon, S., 17–18

Gerbner, George, 4–5, 122

Gladden, Dan, 22, 26

grief, as theme, 9, 94–95, 96

Griffin, Em: *A First Look at Communication Theory*, 41–42

Gross, Larry, 4–5, 122

*Guardian* (UK), 56–57

guns, 29–30, 51–52, 56–57, 59, 110

Gurevitch, Michael, 4

Halberstam, David: *The Best American Sportswriting of the Century*, 18

Hall, Stuart: and false choices, 119; and false completion, 57, 58–59; on ideologies in media, 17; operational

fictions model of, 8, 50–51, 56, 61, 101; and power, 118, 122; pragmatism of, 112

Hamblin, Lizzie, 34–35

Hamblin, Scotty, 34–35

Hanson, Ralph E., 85

Hardt, Hanno, 7

Havel, Vaclav: *Open Letters*, 86

headshots, as incomplete representation, 29–30

Hermida, Alfred, 18

heroes, 13–14, 26–28, 32, 79

heroin use, 35, 93–94, 98–99, 115–16, 118–19, 123

Hill, Kim, 94–95

Hill, Lauryn: *The Miseducation of Lauryn Hill*, 86

history of technology. *See* new media technology history

Huckaby, M. Francyne, 48

Hurd, Ellis, 118

Hussey, Kristin, 60–61

interactions, media shaping, 43, 62, 78, 85, 119

internet, 2, 36, 62, 100, 120

*Interpretative Interactionism* (Denzin), 40

*Jackass* (MTV), 84

Jago, Barbara J., 44, 89

"James" (Merwin), 43

Jaszladany, Hungary, 87

Johnson, Amber Lauren, 47–48

journalism: as active process, 2; changes needed in, 12, 21–22, 92–93, 96, 113–14, 118–19, 120, 121–22; educators helping, 112–13; exposure of problems by, 35; future of, 9, 124–25; importance of, 107–8;

create, 95; and Pulitzer Prize, 34; representative, 95

poetry, 43, 89–90, 111, 121

populations, underrepresented, 21, 78, 92, 118

Poster, Mark: on chaos, 99; and naming, 61; pain in critical theory of, 39, 59, 61, 76, 80, 95–96, 102, 118; pragmatism of, 112; on words, 59–60

Postman, Neil, 17, 38

poststructuralism, 9, 17–18, 75, 97, 107–8, 114, 116, 120, 123

power: and critical theory, 9, 75; journalism influencing, 29–30; of media, 11–12, 50–51, 53–54, 55, 56, 76, 122; and physical disability, 72; and poststructuralism, 17–18; potential of, 51, 105; qualitative research on, 117; relational, 97–98; symbolic, 4–5; of underrepresented groups, 118; views of, 121

power structures: computer as, 120; and critical theory, 5–6; reinforcement of, as general trend, 36, 56–57; reinforcement of, by mediated narration, 8, 16, 21, 27, 31–32, 40, 122–23; reinforcement of, by powerful parties, 119; reinforcement of, by remembrance, 28; resistance to, 36, 97, 123

*The Practice of Everyday Life* (de Certeau), 25–26, 29

prayer, 30, 91

Pressman, Matthew, 69

Pulitzer Prize, 8, 9, 21, 33–34, 40, 92

pushing, and being pushed, 46

qualitative research, 5, 45, 100, 109, 117, 122

Quan-Haase, Anabel, 85

Radnoti, Miklos, 89–90

Rambo, Carol, 63

Rather, Dan, 27

reality, 45, 55, 66, 82, 97, 98, 119. *See also* corporeal reality; narrated reality

*The Real World* (MTV), 86

recollection, 41–42, 45

reconciliation, 47–48, 48–49, 75

religion, 91

remembering, 8, 12, 44–45, 111

reportage: authentic disclosure in, 9, 91–92, 97; broader approach in, 92–93, 101; context revealed by, 33–35; irrelevant remarks in, 31, 73–74; negative impacts revealed by, 94–95; and newness, 118; operational fictions in, 8, 53–54; oversimplification by, 29–30, 31, 57, 60; potential of, 103, 105, 116; and power structure, 27–28; prizewinning, 21, 33; reductive, 26, 58; and sportswriters, 18; superficial, 55–56. *See also* media; news

reporting, 19, 73–74, 92, 93, 97, 98, 108, 115

reportorial work, 92, 101

representation: cultural, 104; eligibility for, 37–40; holistic, 92; importance of, 124; mediated, 17, 46, 72, 82–83, 84, 104; more complete needed, 19, 21, 29–30, 78, 99, 121–22; pluralistic, 79–82; and power, 97, 98; the public and, 3

research. *See* communication research; qualitative research

Rich, Adrienne, 42–43

Richards, Rose, 62

Richardson, Laurel, 65, 87, 89

Rochester MN, 91

Rojas, Rick, 60–61

Roosevelt, Franklin Delano. *See* FDR (Franklin Delano Roosevelt)

Rosenstiel, T.: *The Elements of Journalism*, 108

Rushing, Janice Hocker, 11

Sandy Hook shooting, 49, 50, 59–60

Sandy Hook shooting report: lessons from, 29–30; methodology used in, 51; operational fictions analysis of, 50, 53–56; overview of, 23; retrospective coverage of, 60–61; shortcomings of, 8, 57–58, 115; transcript of, 51–52; video-sharing of, 36–37

school shootings, 12, 49, 51, 56–60, 63, 114, 116

security and freedom, 49, 59, 78, 109–10, 111

self-image, 38, 96

Sender-Message-Channel-Receiver Model (SMCR), 43, 86

sensemaking, 50–51, 81, 82

"Seven Days of Heroin": authentic disclosure in, 91–94; community impact revealed in, 94–97; as good journalism, 8, 21–22, 40; lessons from, 33–36, 97, 99, 100, 103–5; overview of, 25; and technology, 100–103; themes in, 9; video-sharing of, 36–37

Shannon, Claude, 43

Shumate, David, 89

sibling, as theme, 9, 94, 95, 96, 97

silences, 87

Silverstone, Roger, 118

sketches, autoethnographic, 63, 64–65, 89–91

SMCR. *See* Sender-Message-Channel-Receiver Model (SMCR)

*Soccer Shrines* (series), 23, 28–29

social change, 17, 21, 28, 30, 32, 35–36, 40, 99, 124

social constructivism, 42, 108

social media, 51, 62, 63, 85, 98, 118, 124

space: for bodies, 15–16, 20, 39, 46, 76, 83, 90; and everyday life, 90; and lived experience, 65; with place and time, 111; psychic, 6; and reality, 82; as slippery concept, 87; in written communication, 63

spectatorship, 28–29, 62–63. *See also* audiences

sports, significance of, 7–8, 38

sports fans, 23, 28–29, 41

sports heroes, 13–14, 26–28, 32

sportswriters, 18–19

Sproule, J. Michael, 7

Stahl, Roger, 7

Stake, Robert E., 21, 22, 51, 66, 93, 117

stillness, 63–64

story(ies): as assemblage, 50–51; of authors, 1, 91; familiarity of, 12; in future, 82; importance of, 49, 62, 90; of mass media, 89; narration of, 2, 5, 122–23, 124; news, 36–37, 53–54, 67–70, 73, 98, 99, 101; power of, 43, 121; society defined by, 33; as spatial practice, 16; on victims, 12

storying: as active process, 1–3; as continuous, 85; and disabled people, 31; by individuals, 28, 33; of media needed, 21, 40; naming needed in, 57, 58; of new media technology history, 60–61; with time line, 29; understanding from, 26

storytelling, 6, 34, 50–51, 62, 96, 98, 101, 108, 116

strength, 75, 77, 79–80, 84

structuralism, 120

symbols, 4–5, 122

*Pseudo-Memoirs: Life and Its Imitation in Modern Fiction*
by Rochelle Tobias

*The Story of "Me": Contemporary American Autofiction*
by Marjorie Worthington

*Narrative Truthiness: The Logic of Complex Truth in Hybrid (Non)Fiction*
by Annjeanette Wiese

To order or obtain more information on these or other University of Nebraska Press titles, visit nebraskapress.unl.edu.

Lightning Source UK Ltd.
Milton Keynes UK
UKHW010223270821
389562UK00001B/48